THE MARTYR OF THE PONGAS : BEING A MEMOIR OF THE REV. HAMBLE JAMES LEACOCK, LEADER OF THE WEST INDIAN MISSION TO WESTERN AFRICA

Published @ 2017 Trieste Publishing Pty Ltd

ISBN 9780649643998

The Martyr of the Pongas : Being a Memoir of the Rev. Hamble James Leacock, Leader of the West Indian Mission to Western Africa by Henry Caswall

Except for use in any review, the reproduction or utilisation of this work in whole or in part in any form by any electronic, mechanical or other means, now known or hereafter invented, including xerography, photocopying and recording, or in any information storage or retrieval system, is forbidden without the permission of the publisher, Trieste Publishing Pty Ltd, PO Box 1576 Collingwood, Victoria 3066 Australia.

All rights reserved.

Edited by Trieste Publishing Pty Ltd.
Cover @ 2017

This book is sold subject to the condition that it shall not, by way of trade or otherwise, be lent, re-sold, hired out, or otherwise circulated without the publisher's prior consent in any form or binding or cover other than that in which it is published and without a similar condition including this condition being imposed on the subsequent purchaser.

www.triestepublishing.com

HENRY CASWALL

THE MARTYR OF THE PONGAS : BEING A MEMOIR OF THE REV. HAMBLE JAMES LEACOCK, LEADER OF THE WEST INDIAN MISSION TO WESTERN AFRICA

Trieste

THE

MARTYR OF THE PONGAS:

BEING

A Memoir

OF THE

REV. HAMBLE JAMES LEACOCK,

LEADER OF THE WEST INDIAN MISSION
TO WESTERN AFRICA.

BY THE

REV. HENRY CASWALL, D.D.,

VICAR OF FIGHELDEAN, WILTS,
AUTHOR OF "AMERICA AND THE AMERICAN CHURCH," ETC., ETC.,
AND ENGLISH SECRETARY TO THE WEST INDIAN CHURCH
ASSOCIATION FOR THE FURTHERANCE OF THE
GOSPEL IN WESTERN AFRICA.

NEW YORK:
THOMAS N. STANFORD, 637 BROADWAY.
1857

PREFACE.

FEW Missionary heroes have been more remarkable than the man of God whom the West Indian Church is now lamenting. Seldom has more encouraging success attended so brief a career; seldom has a nobler example of self-devotion adorned the records of the extension of Christianity.

The history of such a man, if faithfully told, is well adapted to show the elements which form the able missionary, and to exhibit the modes of action by which, with Divine help, the Gospel may, in our own age, be effectually propagated.

The Author is fully aware of the difficulty of giving due effect to such a history. Yet he has done all that a long and hearty friendship could dictate, to perpetuate the blessed memory of one whom he loved and revered. With the hope of representing him as he really was, he has allowed him to speak for himself whenever opportunity permitted. He has attempted to show the varied connexions and associations of his life, and the origin, as far as it can be traced, of his principles and habits. It is not pretended that Hamble Leacock was in all respects perfect. It is not denied, for example, that he may have been sometimes restless and self-willed, sometimes hasty and over-sensitive, and sometimes mistaken. Yet his failings were generally the result of those · very qualities which constituted the peculiar eminence of his character. His stern and unflinching mind (so tender and holy withal) was doubtless given him that he might *dare* in 'a wonderful way amidst the prejudices of the West Indies, the doctrinal laxity of America, and the heathenism of Africa.

The reader will not see in Mr. Leacock an unamiable abstraction destitute of human feelings and sympathies, but a *man* thoroughly real and unaffected. He will see in him a religion which, though supremely devoted to God, still cherished the impulses of affectionate attachment to friends, relatives, and country; a religion which though profoundly adoring the mysteries of Redemption, was by no means blind to the glories of Providence and Creation. There will be found in it no undue estimate of spiritual condition, no idea of exclusive sanctity or wisdom, no fondness for loud professions, no habit of displaying frames

PREFACE.

and feelings. On the other hand, there will be seen a superiority to the world, practically manifesting itself in the surrender of property and prospects, in the readiness to take a secondary place, and in the cheerful willingness to endure any sacrifice required by justice, truth, and duty.

In the ministry of Christ's Church, it is well that there should be decided varieties of type, and that all should not be formed precisely according to the same model. It is not desirable, for instance, that a clergy designed for service in various nations and climates should be always trained by English Universities and amid the conventionalisms of English society. It will be seen, that the man of God whose life is recorded in the following pages, grew up remote from our fashions of thought, and from the traditionary influences of our Colleges and Cathedrals. Yet it cannot be denied that he was not only a worthy representative of our Reformed Church, but a true specimen of the class of men produced in our distant fields of Christian enterprise. Though his early theological training was, in some respects, defective, he was yet sound in the faith, and inflexible in his adherence to the great bulwarks of orthodoxy. Though firmly attached to the distinctive principles of Episcopacy, he lived in charity with those whose lot had fallen among separatist communities. Believing in the divine origin of the Christian ministry, and upholding a high standard of clerical responsibility, he yet had none of that asceticism which prescribes terms of salvation more severe than are to be found in the Word of God. Faithful in his friendships, firm in his convictions, and sincere in his conversation, he possessed an honest dignity which neither honours nor preferment could have bestowed, and which he maintained throughout all the changes of his eventful life.

Those who have done great things in the world have usually been peculiar persons, different from other men. They have shown uncommon fire, energy, and decision, and, at the same time, have tempered these qualities with knowledge and wisdom. Men of this stamp are not only able to accomplish much, but, amidst the difficulties which surround them, they are susceptible of the choicest encouragements and consolations. Now a mission, properly understood, is no common thing. Persons of an ordinary cast of mind are unfit for such a work. The true missionary cannot be expected to think and feel like those who walk in the beaten track, and, consequently, he will often be reproached as an eccentric person or an enthusiast. Yet his enthusiasm, if such it be, is of the same kind which glowed in the bosoms of the Prophets and

Apostles. It must be carefully distinguished from that enthusiasm which puffs men up with vain conceit, and makes them arrogant, dictatorial, and assuming. Keenly alive to his own personal imperfections, the man who is blessed with this holy fervour looks beyond himself for support, and believing in the power of prayer, habitually and confidently, in all his undertakings, expects strength and succour from above.

In this sense alone Mr. Leacock possessed enthusiasm. But in addition to this, he had qualifications not always combined with a fervid temperament. His habits were regular, economical, active, diligent, and persevering. He was brave and intrepid without being insensible to the real value of life. His piety was of a vigorous and manly character, and at the same time entirely free from that melancholy which has hindered the usefulness of many faithful missionaries. While maintaining habitual communion with his Saviour, he exhibited a genial disposition, which in every place gained him hearty friends. His practical earnestness led him, not to teach people to say certain things or use a certain formula, but to aim at turning them in reality "from darkness unto light, and from the power of Satan unto God."

From early life he had shown the spirit of a mar-

8   PREFACE.

tyr, and his death was in all respects worthy of his
life.   He might probably have escaped dying in
Africa, but he deliberately chose to face "the last
enemy," in the conviction that his decease would be
less injurious to his mission than his abandonment of
his post. Christians like Hamble Leacock are truly
"the chariots of our Israel and the horsemen thereof."
By their deaths they bear the strongest possible testimony against the unbelief of a self-indulgent genera-
tion, and having themselves "fought the good fight,"
and encouraged others to follow their example, they
receive a "crown of glory which fadeth not away."

    Besides exhibiting Mr. Leacock as a missionary,
this little work incidentally affords some insight into
the widely-extended operations of our Reformed
Church. The Episcopate is seen actively engaged in
furthering the salvation of men, not only in England
and the West Indies, but in Eastern and Western
America, and on the pestilential shores of Africa.
Facilities of intercourse and co-operation are disclosed,
which, when more fully employed, will result, with
the Divine blessing, in great and permanent additions
to the Redeemer's kingdom. We may behold an
augury of happier times in the loving sympathy with
which Churchmen of different schools, climates, and
nationalities, have cheered the heart of the veteran
soldier of Christ on the banks of the Pongas.

PREFACE.

The brief services of Mr. Leacock in Africa have been far from fruitless, even independently of the good which he saw accomplished in his lifetime. They have paved the way for new labourers in the same field, who, confidently relying on Providence, may now carry on the work so favourably commenced. We may hope that our Church will continue to exercise an important influence in the conversion of the people of that great continent, in which part of our Lord's infancy was spent, and out of which God was pleased to call his Son. To the West Indian Church in particular this African mission, so manifestly favoured by heaven, will probably become a source of many blessings. In " watering" others she will be herself "refreshed." She has in truth offered unto God, for the sake of the Gospel, one of her own beloved children. Believing that the offering is to Him " a sacrifice acceptable and well-pleasing," we have reason to hope that He will " supply all her need according to his riches in glory by Christ Jesus."

With these prefatory remarks the Author commits this little volume to the blessing of God, and to the favourable consideration of Christian people.

Vicarage, Figheldean,
Epiphany, 1857.

CONTENTS.

CHAPTER I.

Birth and Parentage of Mr. Leacock. Development of his Character. He becomes decidedly religious. Entrance on a Course of Study at Codrington College. His Ordination. His firmness in respect to the Slaves. His Character as a Clergyman. Marriage. Settlement in Nevis. Death of Mrs. Leacock. Effect of an Earthquake. Second Marriage. Removal to the United States, ... 17

CHAPTER II.

Arrival of Mr. Leacock at Lexington, Kentucky. Society in Lexington. Dr. Coit. Dr. Cooke. Amos Cleaver. The Bishop of Kentucky. The Professors. The Southern Planters. Efforts for the Promotion of Religion. Christ-Church. Instruction of the Slaves. Confirmation of Mr. Leacock. He undertakes the charge of Pupils. He is elected Rector of St. Paul's, ... 31

CHAPTER III.

A General Scattering of Mr. Leacock's Friends. He removes to Tennessee. Journey with the Bishop of Tennessee. He accepts a Church at Franklin. Anecdote of him by Mrs. Wheat. He purchases an Estate in New Jersey. Brief connection with a Church at Louisville. His Character as a Preacher and a Pastor. Removal to New Jersey. Settlement during four years at Perth Amboy. Return to the West Indies, . . 42

12   CONTENTS.

CHAPTER IV.

Reasons for his Return. State of Nevis. African practices. Obeah. Mr.
Leacock delivers Lectures against Obeah. Death of the Obeah-man.
Effect of Charms on the African. Return to Barbados. Temporary
Charge of St. Peter's. Death of Amos Cleaver and Dr. Cooke. Mr. Lea-
cock is appointed to the Chapel at Bridgetown. Testimonial of the Pa-
rishioners of St. Peter's. Commencement of efforts in behalf of Africa.
Formation of the Society for the furtherance of the Gospel. Outbreak
of Cholera. Death of Mrs. Leacock, ...   62

CHAPTER V.

Mr. Leacock volunteers to go as a Missionary to Africa. He is accepted,
and is joined by Duport. His Negro Servant desires to accompany him.
Letter to Archdeacon Trew. Arrival in London. He attends a Meeting
of the Church Emigrants' Aid Society. He visits the Crystal Palace.
Visit to Wiltshire—Stonehenge—Salisbury. Meeting of the S. P. G.
His Cheerfulness. Conversation with Young Persons. His views of
Prophecy, of the Church of Rome, and of the Church of England. His
opinion of the Voluntary System. Thankfulness for Mercies. Note on
the Effects of Emancipation in the West Indies, ...   77

CHAPTER VI.

Providential Preparation in Africa for the West Indian Mission. The
Chief Wilkinson introduced. Remarkable Dream in Africa. Mr. Leacock attends various Meetings in the Diocese of Salisbury. He meets
with a Portrait of Mrs. Trimmer. Verses by Mr. Marriott. Mr. Leacock's opinion of the S.P.G. He visits Malvern and the Bishop of Barbados. His Admiration of England. His Feelings in Wells Cathedral.
He embarks at Plymouth for Africa, ...   96

CHAPTER VII.

Voyage of the "Ethiope." Dangerous Storm. Arrival at Madeira. Warm
Reception by a Governor on the African Coast. Arrival at Sierra Leone.
Description of Freetown. Various Opinions as to the Site of the Mission.
Similarity of Sierra Leone to the West Indies. Joy at the Discovery of
Devil-grass. Dr. Bradshaw's advice as to a House. The Niger Consid-
ered. Plaintain Island and John Newton. Further Delay. Inter-
view with the Spanish Consul. Meeting of the Church Missionary
Society, ...   111

CONTENTS. 13

CHAPTER VIII.

When the Episcopate is a Blessing, and when the Reverse. Value of the Episcopate to Sierra Leone. Its Benefits in the West Indies. Rise of the West Indian Church in consequence of the Episcopate. Establishment of the West Indian Mission. Episcopacy acknowledged by Christendom. Greeting to the Bishop of Sierra Leone. Prophetic declaration, ... 126

CHAPTER IX.

Melville Horne on the Qualifications of an African Missionary. The Rio Pongas is mentioned to Mr. Leacock. The Governor promises to send Mr. Leacock to the Pongas in a Steamer. Character of Governor Hill. Meeting with a Mohammedan King. Landing at Tintima. Palaver with Kennyback Ali and King Katty. Description of the Pongas River. Hut at Tintima. Wretched character of the people. Deceitfulness of Kennyback Ali. Mr. Leacock visits him. Encounter with a Mohammedan, ... 136

CHAPTER X.

Events of St. Thomas's Day. Arrival of Lewis Wilkinson. Interview with the chief of Fallangia. Mr. Leacock opens his Ministry among the Heathens. Mr. Wilkinson gives him a Site for a Church, &c. The Missionaries are attacked with Fever. Anxiety of Governor Hill on their Account. He sends a Steamer and removes them to Sierra Leone. They return to Fallangia. John Duport begins to teach. Supplies ordered in England, ... 156

CHAPTER XI.

American Sympathy towards Mr. Leacock. Dr. Coit and the Editor of the "New York Church Journal." The parish at Perth Amboy and the Slaves in Tennessee. Joint Offerings from America and England to Africa. Appointment of an English Secretary. Account of the martyred French Missionaries, ... 171

CHAPTER XII.

The School at Fallangia. Return of Fever. Conversation with Wilkinson. Extent of the Soosoo Language. Need of additional Teachers. Welcome from King Jelloram Fernandez. The Missionaries again taken ill. Con-

CONTENTS.

tinuance of Journal. Duport sent for his health to Sierra Leone. Resemblance of the Negroes of Fallangia to those of Barbados. Conversation with "old Martha." Witchcraft. Second Conversation with "old Martha." Return of Duport. Death of Kennyback Ali. Description of neighboring Chiefs. Agriculture and Animals,　.　.　.　.　181

CHAPTER XIII.

Assurance of King Katty. Miseries of the People. Visit from Mr. Columbini de Wasky. Application from Cassini. Excursion to the Bangalong River. Domingia. Sangha. Farrangeah. Increase of the Congregation under Duport. Journal continued. Relapse of Mr. Leacock. He visits Sierra Leone, and is ordered to return to England. He determines to remain at his Post,　.　.　.　.　.　.　.　206

CHAPTER XIV.

Mr. Leacock's Friends desire him to escape from Africa. Letters to that Effect from Mr. Wilkinson, from the Author, and from the Bishop of Barbados. He appears to recover. His Plans for building. Letter to a Young Person,　.　.　.　.　.　.　.　.　.　.　220

CHAPTER XV.

Satisfactory Progress of the Mission under Duport. Report sent by Duport to Mr. Leacock. Mr. Leacock's Remarks upon it. Favourable Opinion of the Bishop of Sierra Leone respecting it. The Lord's Prayer in Soosoo,　.　.　.　.　.　.　.　.　.　.　230

CHAPTER XVI.

Continued improvement in Mr. Leacock's Health. Letter to his Son. Letters to the Bishop of Barbados. Letter to the Author. Mohammedan Opposition. Assistance from Governor Hill. Contest between Christ and Mohammed. Last Letters of Mr. Leacock,　.　.　.　.　248

CHAPTER XVII.

Articles despatched from England for the Mission. Shipwreck of the "Ida." Death of Mr. Leacock. Letter from the Rev. F. Pocock. Letter

CONTENTS.

from Mr. Duport. Lamentations at Fallangia and Sierra Leone. Letter from the Bishop of Sierra Leone. The mournful news reaches America and the West Indies. Eulogy in the "Barbadian." Concluding Letter from Mr. Duport. Funeral Anthem, ... 260

MEMOIR, ETC

CHAPTER I.

Birth and Parentage of Mr. Leacock. Development of his Character. He becomes decidedly religious. Entrance on a Course of Study at Codrington College. His Ordination. His firmness in respect to the Slaves. His Character as a Clergyman. Marriage. Settlement in Nevis. Death of Mrs. Leacock. Effect of an Earthquake. Second Marriage. Removal to the United States.

HAMBLE JAMES LEACOCK was born at Cluff's Bay, on his father's estate, in the parish of St. Lucy, Barbados, on the 4th of February, 1795. He was the second son of John Wrong Leacock and his wife Rebecca, a sister of Dr. Hudson, of the same parish. He was baptized at home shortly after his birth, but his name did not appear in the parish register at the time, in consequence of the sudden death of the clergyman, a few hours after the ceremony was performed. His family had resided in Barbados about a century and a half, having emigrated from Great Britain in the reign of Charles I. Their respectability and loyalty

18   SLAVERY.

were always above question, and their ancient plate
and coat of arms were retained as badges of their descent from worthy ancestors in the mother country.
Mr. Leacock's father was possessed of a sugar planta-
tion and other similar property, in consequence of
which the subject of our memoir was familiar from
his childhood with many practical details respecting
the growth and manufacture of West India produce.

At this time slavery existed in the islands, and
produced effects in many respects similar to those described in the romances of Mrs. Beecher Stowe. To
slavery, in the abstract, as well as to its abuses, it is
needless to say that the spirit of Christianity is decidedly opposed. Yet it must not be forgotten that in
the West Indies many temperate and well-considered
measures had been adopted, long before emancipation,
tending to relieve the system of many of its horrors.
The African was becoming an object of much sympathy, and the negro race in general escaped that extreme contempt which in other countries is too often
their bitter portion. The slaves in return often showed
themselves faithful and attached dependants, and in
times of trouble manifested a readiness to suffer or die
with their white protectors. Young Leacock grew
up in immediate contact with the subject race, and
learned by experience the surest methods of influ-
encing their conduct.

His own character, like that of others, was probably developed, as to its main features, at an early age.
It may readily be believed that he was always truthful, courageous, and energetic. His temper was no

DEVELOPMENT OF CHARACTER.

doubt severely tried by the harsh schoolmaster under whose care he was placed, yet perhaps the discipline which he underwent was a blessing to him in after life. He acquired all that was essential to the basis of a good education, and became fond of reading useful and instructive books. One of the first of these which made any serious impression on his mind was a volume of Mrs. Trimmer's "Instructive Tales."

In the early formation of his character, we must not omit to notice the peculiar circumstances of his West Indian descent and early associations. He had watched the effect of hurricanes as they swept across his native island, prostrating every resisting substance, uprooting trees, and scattering the materials of the strongest edifices. He had known cannon to be blown from the ramparts, and human beings whirled into the sea. The dwelling inhabited by his family he had seen totally demolished, the last inmate barely escaping before the whole fabric was scattered before the winds. He had gone through the terrors of the earthquake, and had seen the ground undulating like the sea, while men, women, and children were crushed beneath the ruins of their homes. He had seen Barbados covered with the ashes conveyed by the winds from a volcano which burst forth in one of the neighbouring islands. Such events as these had served to predispose his mind to ideas of the grand and terrible, and to fill it with awful thoughts of the dread majesty and irresistible power of the Almighty.

Through divine grace he was preserved in his youth from the contagion of vice, and always maintained a high character among his equals. Still he had not become decidedly religious, nor made that complete surrender of himself to the love of Christ which constitutes the essence of a devout life. At length, after the days of boyhood, while on a visit to a neighbouring island, his convictions found at the same time their expression and confirmation in a remarkable dream. The future state of the just was represented to him in all its blessedness, and he seemed to hear the harps of gold and the general chorus of the redeemed. Again he beheld in his dream the miseries of the condemned, and his ear seemed to thrill with their groans of anguish as they endured the never-ending penalty of their transgressions. He awoke with the firm conviction that thenceforth he must strive with all his might to enter in at the strait gate, and labour to the utmost of his capacity in promoting upon earth the knowledge of divine truth. From this period he became a very decided Christian, constantly subordinating time to eternity, and living under the influence of the things which are not seen.

The same miserable policy which formerly kept the American colonies without bishops had prevailed up to this period in the West Indies. In consequence of the destitution of episcopal superintendence, Mr. Leacock had not hitherto received Confirmation. The means of a good and Christian education, however, were not wanting, even in Barbados. Codrington College had been founded in 1710 by the worthy General whose name it bears, and who had given it by will his two plantations in Barbados and part of the island of Barbuda. This property had been held in trust by the Society for Propagating the Gospel "to erect a college in Barbados, and to maintain a convenient number of professors and scholars who are to be obliged to study and practise physic and chirurgery, as well as divinity, that by the apparent usefulness of the former to all mankind, they may both endear themselves to the people, and have the better opportunity of doing good to men's souls whilst they are taking care of their bodies." At this institution, then nothing more than a grammar school, and under the care of the Rev. Mark Nicholson, formerly of Queen's College, Oxford, Mr. Leacock entered as a student. He did not aim at eminence as a classical scholar, but became familiar with English literature and other useful branches of knowledge.

On quitting Codrington College he kept a private school in Speightstown for several years, and afterwards the public school of his native parish. Many of his pupils are still living, and continue to love and revere his memory. In the midst of his engagements he constantly allotted certain portions of his time to the study of the Scriptures, in which he became a proficient.

In the year 1824 a happier era dawned on the Barbadian Church. In that year Dr. Coleridge was consecrated bishop of Barbados and the Leeward Islands, and on the 30th of January, 1825, landed in his new diocese. Bishop Coleridge soon afterwards licensed Mr. Leacock as a reader or catechist for his native parish of St. Lucy, of which the Rev. W. M.

Harte was at that time rector. On the 6th of January, 1826, after studying divinity under Mr. Harte, he was ordained a deacon, and on the 18th of October in the same year he was admitted to the priesthood at St. John's Church, in one of the country parishes, his confirmation being still unaccountably neglected.

While continuing his connexion with Mr. Harte and the parish of St. Lucy, he fully established his character as a zealous and uncompromising Christian. At that time the teaching of the slave population in the West Indies was a most unpopular measure. Mr. Harte was publicly prosecuted because he boldly affirmed his right to instruct all persons, bond as well as free, living within the limits of his parish. He was charged with preaching an offensive sermon on Easter-day, 1827, and "with disgraceful conduct while administering the Lord's Supper." The truth was that Mr. Harte permitted a vacant space at the Lord's Table to be occupied by blacks, who knelt down at the same time with some white members of the congregation. In allowing this, Mr. Harte was supposed to be teaching "doctrines of equality, inconsistent with the obedience due to masters and with the policy of the island." The planters resolved to take the matter into their own hands, and expressed their determination to refuse Mr. Harte and Mr. Leacock admission into their estates, and to prevent as much as possible all intercourse between them and their slaves. They desired the bishop to remove Mr. Harte, who they said "had deservedly lost the confidence, respect, and regard of every white inhabitant of the parish."

FIRMNESS IN RESPECT TO THE SLAVES. 23

Owing to the admirable wisdom of the bishop, the people were ultimately brought to a better mind, and the immediate expulsion of two devoted servants of God was averted. Mr. Leacock never yielded for a moment to the popular prejudice, but acted in full accordance with the views and wishes of his rector, in regarding the humblest negro as a part of his ministerial charge. Those who know not the violence of feeling which then existed on the subject can form no correct opinion of the strength of character required to resist the will and combat the inveterate prejudices of almost all the influential inhabitants of the colony.

A venerable divine, who was acquainted with Mr. Leacock at this period, still bears admiring testimony to the zeal and determination constantly manifested by him in his ministerial duties of every kind. Courage and decision were indeed striking points in his character, together with a certain impulsiveness which often led him to act and speak vigorously on the spur of the moment. Like other inhabitants of tropical climates, the earthquake and hurricane seemed, in a manner, to have entered into his constitution. In him, however, it was seen that West Indian fervour, when sanctified by divine grace, is as effectual an instrument of good as the coolness of the Englishman, the shrewdness of the Scot, or the enterprise of the American. His religion was of a thoroughly warm and glowing character, far removed from the frigid zones of mere formalism and precision. He cared not for verbal subtleties or nice disputations; but firmly believing the grand central verities of the Christian

Faith, he ardently loved the Redeemer on account of what He had done and suffered, and was willing to perish for his sake. When he rebuked vice, he did it with an awful earnestness which made the sinner tremble and turn pale. With a few words he swept away all his refuges of lies and set before him the real horrors of his position. When he comforted the sorrowful or penitent, on the other hand, nothing could exceed the beautiful tenderness with which he applied the promises and encouragements of the Gospel.

His mode of reading and speaking was vividly dramatic, and often accompanied by expressive action. The Scriptures, when read by him, became, as it were, a new book. The awful images of Ezekiel and of the Apocalypse were made to appear plain and distinct, so that the hearer perceived depths in the word of God of which he had been previously ignorant. He impressed divine truth on the minds of others because he had first been deeply impressed by it himself.

His conduct was consistent with his faith and teaching. With a heart fully alive to heavenly things, he was comparatively careless as to worldly interests. Money, luxuries, and even comforts were lightly esteemed by him, and he regarded all solicitude about such matters unworthy of a candidate for eternal life. Yet he always maintained a respectable appearance, and showed himself sensitively punctilious in the discharge of pecuniary obligations. In his worldly transactions he was a model of simplicity and godly sincerity.

Mr. Leacock had married a distant relation, the only daughter of Dr. Leacock, of Barbados, by whom he became the father of several children. Being the owner of many slaves in right of his wife, he set them all free at a great sacrifice and expense, since the manumissions had to be obtained from England. His uncompromising opposition to slavery was still disapproved of by his countrymen. He therefore left his native isle, and in December, 1826, immediately after his ordination to the Priesthood, was sent by Bishop Coleridge to St. Vincent. Soon afterwards the bishop removed him to Nevis, where he was appointed rural dean, and succeeded the Rev. Mr. Parham at Charlestown as rector of St. Paul's, one of the five parishes of the island. Here he built a house and established his wife and family comfortably. After a short time, however, Mrs. Leacock and one of his children died, and he was made to feel the vanity of all earthly consolations.

Nevis is a beautiful little spot, consisting of a single mountain, rising like a cone in an easy ascent from the sea, the whole circumference not exceeding twenty-four miles. It evidently owes its origin to some volcanic eruption, for near the summit there is a crater which contains a hot spring strongly impregnated with sulphur. The population of the island amounted during Mr. Leacock's incumbency to about ten thousand, of whom not more than six hundred were whites. Here Mr. Leacock laboured with char-

2

acteristic energy, establishing schools and promoting the catechetical instruction of the blacks. The evils with which he contended were of a fearful character, polygamy and other forms of licentiousness being too generally prevalent. In due time, however, he found his labours rewarded by a marked improvement in the religion and morals of the people. The following event contributed to this happy result :—

Nevis, like Barbados, is within the sphere of devastating earthquakes, and between the 8th of February and the 27th of March, 1833, it was terribly shaken, together with St. Kitt's and others of the Leeward Islands. In Nevis the populace were so alarmed that they flocked to the places of worship at all hours of the day. In Charlestown they supplicated Mr. Leacock to open his church that they might there find the security which was elsewhere denied them. Contrary to the prognostications of some worldly-minded scoffers, the church did not fall. The poor negroes crowded it at all hours of the day, beseeching Mr. Leacock to pray for them. It is a fact, attested by eye-witnesses of the highest credit, that a great and abiding change was wrought upon the inhabitants. They who never went to church before, now attended devoutly, and continued to do so afterwards ; and many whose lives had been anything but Christian became decidedly religious, under the terror arising from the earthquake, improved by the faithful teaching of the man of God. Like the gaoler at Philippi, they asked, "What must we do to be saved?" like Paul and Silas, he answered, "Believe

EFFECT OF AN EARTHQUAKE. 27

in the Lord Jesus Christ, and thou shalt be saved."
One of Mr. Leacock's parishioners, a lady of respectability, was reading the 24th chapter of St. Matthew
when the first shock was felt. She had just read the
7th verse, " and there shall be famines, and pesti-
lences, and earthquakes, in divers places," when the
house was shaken violently. She immediately fell
from her seat and was taken up insensible, in which
condition she remained some time. At St. Kitt's,
there were similar instances of violent mental impressions, though a party who were dancing at a public
ball, and felt the room tremble from the shock, still
continued their dance. So different is the effect of
these tremendous visitations according to the character of the persons concerned and of those who influence them.

A contemporary writer, after alluding to Mr. Leacock's faithful labours at this time, remarked as
follows :—

" Whatever the infidel or free-thinker (or rather
no-thinker) may say to the contrary about impressions
on weak minds and so forth, the believer cannot fail
to recognize in these narratives a proof of that principle, upon which every *operative* clergyman (to bor-
ow a cant expression of the day) will sooner or later
stumble, viz. : that the Almighty seems oftentimes to
send visitations of his power to a mass of people, as
well as to an individual, for the purpose of opening a
door to the preaching of the Gospel, where, perhaps,
sin had closed up every avenue to exhortation and
'the common method of teaching."

SECOND MARRIAGE.

While residing in Nevis, Mr. Leacock married Mrs. Beard, a most amiable widow lady, who admirably fulfilled the duties of a mother to his surviving son and daughter. Having no children of her own, she devoted herself to the good and charitable works which lie within the appropriate province of a clergyman's wife. She did even more, often visiting distant parts of the island with the object of conveying relief and good advice to sick persons and others who requested her assistance. She was in all respects a help meet for the earnest-minded man who had chosen her as his companion, and by her gentle influence and thoughtful consideration for the wants of others, she greatly increased the sphere of his usefulness. But their days of labour at Nevis were drawing to a close.

Some uneasiness had arisen between Bishop Coleridge and Mr. Leacock, in consequence of certain public proceedings in which the latter associated himself with members of the Methodist connexion. The bishop had also been annoyed by Mr. Leacock's refusal to sign testimonials in behalf of an applicant whom he conscientiously believed to be unfit for the holy ministry. It is, however, worthy of note that this person, who was afterwards ordained, wrote a letter at a subsequent time to Mr. Leacock to *thank* him for his conduct in this respect.

There were also troubles of a different kind. At this period the negro population in the West Indies was in an unsettled and sometimes in an insurrectionary state. Discussions were going forward in the

British Parliament which held out prospects of emancipation at no distant date. In the meanwhile property of all kinds was rapidly depreciating, and it was generally supposed by respectable white persons that the islands would soon cease to be tenable by those of European origin, and must be wholly given over, like St. Domingo, to the African race. Mr. Leacock and his relations generally shared more or less in these anticipations.

In 1832 his brother, a clergyman of Jamaica, visited the United States, and in the course of his rambles happened to form some acquaintance with the State of Kentucky. His early ideas of the Kentuckians were dissipated by the intelligent and polished society among which he was hospitably received. He was pleased with the agreeable climate of this region, its general salubrity, and its freedom from hurricanes and earthquakes. In addition to all this, he found the slave population quiet and far from dangerous, and felt convinced that he could in Kentucky educate a family in greater security than in the colonies of which he was a native.

Emancipation, in the unsatisfactory form of an apprenticeship, took place on the 1st of August, 1834. In 1835, the two Leacocks, with their wives and children, and other near relations, bade farewell to the West Indies, and after a favourable voyage landed in New York. Here their emancipated negro servants were informed of their freedom, and were reminded that in going to Kentucky they would be returning to a land of slavery. They determined, however, to

REMOVAL TO THE UNITED STATES.

proceed, and one old negro woman expressed the feelings of the others, when she said with hearty good feeling, " Wherever massa goes, there I go too."

Travelling in those days in America was a different thing from what it is at present. The whole party proceeded by Philadelphia, and by a tedious journey across the Alleghany mountains to the West. Accustomed to islands generally smaller than the Isle of Wight, they now saw before them a vast and apparently unlimited extent of fertile territory, rapidly filling up with inhabitants. They entered Kentucky, a country as large as Ireland, and containing a population at that time of about seven hundred thousand, of whom two hundred and fifty thousand were negro slaves. Finally their land journey of nearly a thousand miles was completed, and they established themselves in the pleasant city of Lexington, where the Church people were prepared to give them a hearty welcome.

CHAPTER II.

Arrival of Mr. Leacock at Lexington, Kentucky. Society in Lexington. Dr. Coit. Dr. Cooke. Amos Cleaver. The Bishop of Kentucky. The Professors. The Southern Planters. Efforts for the Promotion of Religion. Christ-Church. Instruction of the Slaves. Confirmation of Mr. Leacock. He undertakes the charge of Pupils. He is elected Rector of St. Paul's.

On the 15th of July, 1835, the Leacocks arrived in Lexington. Although in latitude 38°, nearly fifteen degrees from the tropics, they found the heat of the summer intense, and greatly missed the sea-breezes of their native islands. I was, at that time, residing in Lexington, as professor in the Episcopal Theological Seminary, and as minister of Christ-Church during the absence of the bishop. I lost no time in forming an acquaintance with the new-comers, and on the following Sunday, at my request, Mr. Hamble Leacock occupied the pulpit. After hearing his discourse, I felt persuaded that among the impulsive and warm-hearted people of Kentucky so fervid a preacher would have great opportunities of doing good.

SOCIETY IN LEXINGTON.

At the period of which I speak there was much of an interesting character in the society of Lexington. As the life of every man is more or less influenced by his associates, it seems proper in this place to give some account of those with whom Mr. Leacock lived for several years on the most intimate terms.

There is in Lexington an institution founded and amply endowed by the State, and denominated Transylvania University. The principal building occupies an eminence, upon which its spacious Grecian portico shows to considerable advantage. Like other State institutions of the kind in America, this university is not attached to any particular religious denomination, and the president and professors are at liberty to exert whatever doctrinal influences they may individually prefer upon the minds of the students. Sometimes, in the Kentucky University, Unitarian influences had predominated, and sometimes Presbyterian. During the whole period of Mr. Leacock's residence in Lexington, Churchmanship was in the ascendant, the president of the institution being the Rev. Dr. Coit. Dr. Coit represented that large class of American Episcopalians who have been led into the Church by honest conviction. Of a family once partly Quaker and partly Puritan, he was himself an able expounder of the peculiar principles which separate us from sectarian bodies. He had already shown himself skilful in polemic theology, and the Puritans in particular had often felt his power in controversial engagements. As a native of New England, he was

DR. COOKE. 33

different in temperament from our West Indian friend, but not less earnest, and probably not less successful, in maintaining the cause which was equally dear to both.

Connected with the university there was also a Medical College, which boasted an array of distinguished names, some of which have acquired an European reputation, while all were possessed of at least respectability in the West. Among the medical professors there was one who deserved the peculiar gratitude of all earnest Churchmen. This was Dr. Cooke, Professor of the Theory and Practice of Medicine.

Dr. Cooke, though a native of the United States, was of West Indian origin, his parents having removed from the island of Bermuda. He commenced practice as a physician in Virginia, and in 1827 removed to Lexington, where his career as a professor is described by his biographer* as one great and almost unexampled triumph. Although troubled with a slight impediment of speech, the earnestness of his manner, the depth of his convictions, the singleness of his purpose, the simplicity and comprehensiveness of his views, and his intense devotion to truth, made him the most interesting of companions.

It was during this active period of his life that Dr. Cooke was called upon to turn his great powers to another and very different. field of research. For many years previous to 1829 he had been a zealous

---

* Rev. Dr. Craik, of Louisville.

2*

member of the Methodist body. The causes that induced him to abandon this connexion, and to attach
himself to the American Episcopal Church, are before
the public in the introduction to his work, republished
in England, on the "Invalidity of Presbyterian Ordination." In prosecuting his inquiry he had ran-
sacked the University Library, rich in many old
books, and all the private libraries within his reach.
The examination was begun and prosecuted with all
the ardour of a strong and enthusiastic nature. Only
four hours were allowed for sleep; one hour was
given to the accustomed lecture before the medical
class; the shortest time possible to meals, and the
rest of the twenty-four devoted to the absorbing
inquiry upon which he had entered. To relieve the
brain from the effects of this intense and unremitted
application, and to keep his mind in the highest
state of free and vigorous action, he several times
bled himself during the six weeks of this remarkable
investigation. At the end of that time his conviction was complete, and the materials of that conviction, soon afterwards embodied in the essay above
mentioned, were accumulated and ready for future
use. He immediately connected himself with the
Episcopal Church, and neither he nor his family ever
after attended any other place of worship. With all
the force and enthusiasm of his character, Dr. Cooke
then applied himself to the work of raising up the
Church in Kentucky. It was in a great measure
through his persevering efforts that the Rev. B. B.
Smith was consecrated bishop of the diocese in 1832,

and the Theological Seminary established two years afterwards.

It may readily be imagined that Mr. Leacock found much in Dr. Cooke congenial with his own earnest character. A friendship was formed between them, which was dissolved only by the death of Dr. Cooke in 1853. The intercourse was beneficial to both parties. On the one hand, the fervent piety of the clergyman warmed the heart of the physician; on the other hand, the physician's researches into ecclesiastical history enlightened the mind of the clergyman on many points which hitherto he had but slightly considered. Mr. Leacock had readily acquiesced in episcopacy, as the established system in that portion of the British dominions in which he had been educated. But now in the United States he was made to perceive that religious institutions, to be permanent, require a foundation deeper than an "establishment" can afford. Dr. Cooke's argument assured him that no ministerial authority can be justly esteemed valid which can be traced to any origin short of Christ's commission to the Apostles. He was thus led to the idea of a regular line of ecclesiastical descent, which his new friend enabled him to trace as a matter of fact through the history of the Church, from the earliest institution of Christianity to the present English and American episcopate.

In addition to Drs. Coit and Cooke, Mr. Leacock and myself had another friend in the Rev. Amos Cleaver, once a Baptist minister in England, but then a devoted Churchman, acting as missionary in a

36 AMOS CLEAVER AND THE BISHOP.

town within a moderate distance of Lexington. Mr. Cleaver had found in this place not more than one or two families of Episcopalians; yet upon this foundation he had resolved to commence operations. He purchased a piece of ground, and with his own hands, assisted by his two sons and a hired negro, began erecting the walls of a church, officiating on Sundays for the benefit of a mere handful of people in the Court House. His private means soon failing, he performed several tours through the United States, and by dint of hard begging succeeded in raising five thousand dollars, with which he erected a handsome place of worship, now occupied by a comparatively large congregation. After seeing this work completed, Mr. Cleaver went as a missionary into Mississippi, where in 1853 he died a martyr to duty, having caught the yellow fever while faithfully attending to his flock during the prevalence of that devastating pestilence.

The bishop of the diocese was necessarily often absent, but when at home he contributed greatly to the intellectual society of Lexington. His philosophical views on various subjects, combined with considerable originality in his style of thought, rendered his conversation as interesting as it was instructive. He had long been an earnest friend of the missionary cause, even in times when the American Church was too negligent of her duty in this respect.

Besides the above, we were more or less acquainted with the various professors in the university, the medical and theological students, the intelligent citizens of Lexington, and a somewhat diversified selection of Baptist, Methodist, and Presbyterian ministers. Not unfrequently we met the pastor of the Roman Catholic Church, and his able assistant, the Rev. Mr. McGill, a native Kentuckian, and now the Roman Catholic Bishop of Richmond.

During the heat of summer the seven thousand inhabitants of Lexington received an annual augmentation in the numerous wealthy planters and their families, who came up to escape the still greater heat of the States further south. Among them was always a considerable portion of refined and cultivated persons, whose minds had been enlarged and improved by foreign travel. Many of these were sincere members of the Church, who strove to do their duty to their negro dependants, and to make them as virtuous and happy as their circumstances would admit.

But in Western America there are multitudes who, from the want of a generally accepted system of external as well as internal religion, grow up in practical heathenism, unbaptized and unbelieving. Sectarian divisions augment the tendency to negation of truth ; and it generally happens that a large portion of a clergyman's efforts are directed against open infidelity. Our friend Dr. Coit was eminently useful in this particular branch of service. He delivered from time to time admirable lectures to the medical students and others, in which he proved the divine origin of the Christian religion, the genuineness of the Scriptures, and the inspired character of the

38 EFFORTS FOR THE PROMOTION OF RELIGION.

sacred writers. Dr. Cooke, in his professional instructions, availed himself of frequent opportunities for demonstrating the existence of a Deity, his wisdom, goodness, and power. Mr. Leacock, in his sermons and exhortations took a different line, and addressing himself directly to the heart and conscience, attacked the strongest holds of unbelief. Taking it for granted that Christianity was divine, and divinely adapted to the human soul, his great aim was to present it in all the fulness of its claims and in all the greatness of its sanctions.

Our church was a spacious building, accommodating about six hundred persons. At the time of Mr. Leacock's arrival we were much engaged in promoting the Greek mission-school which Mr. and Mrs. Hill had recently established at Athens, and which has since become a powerful instrument of good. For the advancement of missions in foreign parts as well as in Kentucky itself, we had weekly collections, which amounted to about 135*l.* in the course of a year. A "Ladies' Sewing Society," in which Mrs. Leacock took an active and efficient part, was one of the means of swelling this fund. The ladies assembled usually at the house of some clergyman, who, as their work advanced, read to them interesting details of missionary progress.

Mr. Leacock found in Kentucky but few opportunities of doing special service to the negro race. Unlike the West Indies, he found the slaves in this region almost wholly disconnected with the Church, and living under a system necessarily adverse to

INSTRUCTION OF SLAVES. 39

mental and moral culture. The greater part of them were predestinarian Baptists, and addicted to a noisy and exciting form of religion. Besides this, the authorities had been alarmed by the emancipation going forward in the British possessions. Strict measures were now adopted to prevent entirely the somewhat rare practice of teaching slaves to read. With the help of our theological students, we had succeeded in assembling about seventy-five young negroes in a Sunday school. But when it was understood that something more than oral instruction was attempted, the mayor of the city requested us to desist from so dangerous a proceeding, as he felt himself unable to protect us against a mob, which in a moment of excitement might level our seminary with the dust.

Meantime Dr. Cooke was augmenting his library by the importation from Europe of the best editions of the Fathers and other theological works of value. He acted in our seminary as professor of the History and Polity of the Church, occasionally delivering lectures on these subjects to our students. On the 11th of June, 1835, he was elected by the Diocesan Convention of Kentucky as one of its lay deputies to the General Convention which assembled that year in Philadelphia. Mr. Leacock was much interested in this appointment, and offered up many prayers in regard to the proceedings of the great triennial assembly of the American Church. Dr. Cooke on this occasion startled the quiet conservatism of the members of that body, by introducing a resolution providing for the immediate election and consecration of a bishop for each State and Territory in the United States in which there was no bishop. This sweeping and thorough proposition was partially acted upon at the time, by the appointment of two missionary bishops for the West, one of whom, Bishop Kemper, still continues, in a vigorous old age, to perform his apostolic duties throughout a vast extent of territory. Ultimately the Church awoke to a sense of her high calling; and at present there is no part of the United States without its bishop.

Soon after Dr. Cooke's return from the Convention, the winter set in with its usual severity. Although we were so far to the southward the frost was often as sharp as in Canada, the thermometer being forty or fifty degrees below freezing. Our West Indian friends suffered severely, and, for the first time in his life, Mr. Hamble Leacock saw the phenomena of ice and snow. During a part of the winter, sleighs were travelling about as in the Northern States and colonies, and Christmas appeared in a garb worthy of its ancient English character. About this time the bishop held a confirmation in Christ-Church. Mr. Leacock resolved to fulfil the duty which had been neglected in his youth, and came forward together with a number of young persons to receive the imposition of the bishop's hands. He felt that, in so doing, he was not only setting a valuable example to others, but that he was placing himself in the way of receiving a blessing to his own soul.

He was at this time engaged in tuition, having returned for a brief space to the occupation of his earlier life. His pupils were sincerely attached to him, and his deportment towards them was in all respects that of a father. In the summer of 1836 a new congregation or "parish," denominated St. Paul's, having been commenced in Lexington, Mr. Leacock was elected rector, with a moderate compensation. The University Chapel was lent to the new congregation, in view of the possible erection of a church. The instrumental music was led by Mrs. Leacock, the body of the worshippers joining in the chants, psalms, and hymns, usual in the American Church. The subject of this memoir seemed again to have found his proper place, and soon showed himself the fervent preacher and the efficient pastor of former times.

CHAPTER III.

A General Scattering of Mr. Leacock's Friends. He removes to Tennessee. Journey with the Bishop of Tennessee. He accepts a Church at Franklin. Anecdote of him by Mrs. Wheat. He purchases an Estate in New Jersey. Brief connection with a Church at Louisville. His Character as a Preacher and a Pastor. Removal to New Jersey. Settlement during four years at Perth Amboy. Return to the West Indies.

OUR pleasant ecclesiastical society in Lexington was not destined to a long duration. Dr. Cooke's biographer remarks with much justice, that " the effort then making for the extension of the Church in Kentucky involved too much centralization. The large ecclesiastical force collected in Lexington was utterly disproportionate to the condition and strength of the diocese. It was an enormous head without a body. If Dr. Cooke and his fellow-Churchmen could have brought from the East a band of itinerant preachers, and sent them with the bishop at their head through the State, gathering up and organizing into congregations the Episcopalian families which were thickly scattered over the whole country, the result would have been different. Unhappily this policy was not pursued in Kentucky, and the consequence is that we

A SCATTERING OF FRIENDS. 43

still mourn over the deplorable weakness of the Church in this diocese."

Historical veracity makes it necessary to add that difficulties of a peculiar kind had now overshadowed the bright early days of the Church of Kentucky. A controversy involving many personal considerations had arisen, which finally involved the clergy and laity together with the Bishop and the Diocesan Convention. The result of the whole was an episcopal trial, at which Bishops Kemper, McIlvaine, and Mc-Coskry presided. Throughout the entire course of these painful proceedings the conduct of Mr. Leacock was in complete accordance with the truthfulness and integrity of his character.

Dr. Coit, meeting with considerable discouragement in the management of the State University, resigned his appointment in 1837, and returning to the East became the pastor of a congregation in the pleasant village of New Rochelle, on Long Island Sound, not far from New York. About the same time the admirable position and rapid growth of Louisville induced the majority of the medical professors to look to that city as the most eligible place in the western country for a great medical school. Accordingly Dr. Cooke removed from Lexington to Louisville, and united with four other scientific gentlemen in founding the medical institute in that city, now known as the Medical Department of the University of Louisville. He continued to teach in this school until its prosperity was placed beyond the reach of competition. Mrs. Polk purchased his valuable ecclesiastical library, at a price of several thousand dollars, and presented it to her husband, the Bishop of Louisiana.

Although highly respected by those who were intimately acquainted with him, Dr. Cooke never attained to popularity. He constantly manifested thorough indifference to public opinion, and stern intolerance of error and flippancy. He threw his great truths before the world, and used no further care to commend or introduce them. He took it for granted that every man would be as devout a worshipper of truth as himself, and was at little pains to conceal his contempt for those who seemed to make truth a secondary consideration. As a necessary consequence Dr. Cooke had many enemies.

Mr. Leacock's brother had quitted Lexington, having purchased an estate at some distance in the country. Several of his relations had returned from Kentucky to the West Indies, where they found that, notwithstanding the apprenticeship system, it was still possible for white persons to exist. Nearly at the same time with Drs. Coit and Cooke, I quitted the diocese of Bishop Smith, and accepted, at Bishop Kemper's invitation, the charge of a rising congregation in the free State of Indiana. In consequence of ill health, I retained this position little more than a year, and in 1838 removed with my family to the healthy North, and took up my residence on British territory, in the loyal colony of Upper Canada. Before parting from Mr. Leacock, I gave him a copy of Thomas à Kempis, with which he was greatly delighted, and which, except his Bible, he valued above all the books in his possession.

In consequence of these and other removals, Mr. and Mrs. Leacock felt themselves solitary, and having no local ties to bind them to Lexington, began to contemplate another change. Mrs. Leacock wrote as follows, in June, 1837 :—

"Another thing which has damped my spirits and rendered me unfit for writing, is that our friend J—— has left us. She went on Monday with Mrs. Coit and her little ones. Dr. Cooke and his family have also taken their departure. Mrs. Cooke and the girls went yesterday, in their private carriage, and the good doctor has this instant started in the car with all his servants. Lexington looks deserted. It makes me melancholy whenever I think of the many excellent friends who have left it, and who in all probability we shall never meet again on earth. I almost wish our turn had come ; but it strikes me we shall·be the last to move."

Within half a year from the date of this letter the expected change had taken place, and Mr. Leacock, at Bishop Otey's invitation, removed southward, into the adjoining State of Tennessee. He spent some time in travelling with the good bishop throughout his extensive diocese, and found in him a cordial friend, a man thoroughly after his own heart, and an edifying and instructive companion. As the two men of God rode together on horseback, they engaged in conversation on noble and elevated subjects, and sometimes made the forests echo to the unwonted sound of their chants and hymns.

Having taken charge, at the bishop's request, of the parish of Franklin, he found himself again engaged in that ministerial work which had always been his delight. Yet his success did not altogether equal his expectations, and certainly fell short of what he had experienced in Nevis. Writing to me on the 5th of February, 1838, he spoke of having innumerable calls on his time, and added as follows :—

"I am getting on tolerably well. Franklin is a charming little place, and if the Lord will bless my labours I shall be happy. The people are friendly and kind ; but I want to see *grace*. I long once more to hear the cry, 'What must I do to be saved?' Remember us affectionately to your dear wife, and may the Lord abundantly bless you in your labours and in your family."

Mrs. Selina Wheat, the wife of a clergyman then residing in Tennessee, has kindly supplied me with the following interesting sketch of Mr. Leacock :—

"During his residence in Tennessee, Mr. Leacock, as was generally required of the clergy of that day, had to do much missionary or itinerant work for the Church. After a Sunday's service in Clarksville, he was returning to his home in Franklin, when he was obliged by illness to stop at our house in Nashville. He had travelled all day, on horseback, under an oppressive sun, and having had a severe chill he was now burning with fever. He was unable to dismount without assistance. My husband and son carried him

in their arms to his room, and we immediately sent
for a physician. As soon as it could be done, a foot-
bath, which we knew to be peculiarly refreshing to
him, was prepared; and my husband, himself taking
off his shoes and stockings, began to bathe his feet.
As I was, at the moment, making a cooling application
to his head, I observed Mr. Leacock weeping passion-
ately. Alarmed, I begged to know the cause. 'Was
he more ill than we supposed? Should we send for his
wife? What was the matter? Why did he weep?'
With some effort he became more calm, and confessed
—would you believe it?—that he wept because my
husband was performing so menial an office for him.
'Why! Mr. Leacock,' I said, 'would not you do as
much for him?' 'Oh yes, certainly,' he replied, and
then, no doubt recurring to the incident in the Gospels,
he added, 'not his feet only, but his hands and his head.'

"A few weeks after this, he was called to be *our*
comforter; for we had been bereaved of a precious
child. He remained with us several days after the
funeral, taking my husband's duty on the following
Sunday, and oh, how well I remember his untiring
efforts to console us? Once, in the anguish of my
grief, I said to him, 'Oh! Mr. Leacock, we little
thought when you left us so lately that you would be
called to perform this sad office for us—that I should
lose my Heber!' He was pacing the floor, and suddenly turning upon me, he said very earnestly, 'Are
you a Christian mother, and say that Heber is *lost?*
Oh, say not *lost;* but only *gone before.* Do not let
me hear you use such language again. You shall go

to him, if you meekly submit yourself to your heavenly Father's will—but say not again that your child is lost.' I confess his stern rebuke did more to calm my grief than all his previous words of gentle remonstrance.

"We once again saw him and his model wife, in a great trial of a very different kind, after they had lost the greater part of their property by the failure of a friend. I never can forget their Christian fortitude and magnanimous forbearance towards the wrong-doer, who had so cruelly disappointed them. 'God will provide,' they said; 'yes, and He will bring good out of this evil. We can but pray for him who has done us this great wrong.' Not a word of severity, hardly of reproach, did I hear from those holy lips."

The following letter addressed to me by Bishop Otey completes the record of Mr. Leacock's ministry in Tennessee :—

> "Ebenezer, near Memphis, Tennessee,
> Dec. 8, 1856.

"Rev. and dear Sir,

"I feel a melancholy interest in complying with your request to furnish any particulars I may possess connected with the ministry of our late dearly-beloved and lamented brother, the Rev. Hamble J. Leacock, while resident in this diocese. These particulars are not many, being collected chiefly, such as they are, from notices scattered through my annual reports to the Diocesan Convention.

"He was canonically transferred from the diocese of Kentucky to that of Tennessee on the fifth day of

LETTER FROM BISHOP OTEY. 49

January, 1838. You are yourself aware of the unhappy difficulties which disturbed the peace of the Church in Kentucky for several years previous to this time, in consequence of which Mr. Leacock and his brother were induced to seek situations in this State. Hamble took charge of St. Paul's, Franklin, to the rectorship of which he was formally invited by the Vestry. In his first parochial report, he says with characteristic modesty, 'The rector sees no decided testimony that his labours have been successful; yet he hopes that they have not been altogether in vain. He trusts there are a few who maintain, in secret, a faithful adherence to Christ, and like plants in the wilderness blossom unseen, and diffuse their fragrance unperceived, except by Him who seeth all things.'

"As evidence of the estimate in which he was held by his brethren, it may be mentioned that, at the Convention held six months after his removal into the diocese, he was elected a member of the Standing Committee and a trustee of the General Theological Seminary.

" The next notice of him is taken from my annual report for the next year, in these words: 'The Rev. H. J. Leacock preached an effective and impressive sermon on the duties of the ministry, on the occasion of ordaining two deacons to the priesthood and a candidate to the diaconate.' This took place at Clarksville during the session of the Convention. His manner was very impressive and earnest, and few who heard him then, or at other times, are likely to have forgotten the power with which he spake.

3

LETTER FROM BISHOP OTEY.

"It was during the years 1838 and 1839 that he accompanied me on a visitation of the greater part of my diocese. Our journeyings together on horseback gave me good opportunities to learn the character of this truly *great*, because he was a truly *good*, man. It was here that he opened his heart, and uncovered the deep well-springs and fountains of the spiritually-minded man, overflowing with love to Christ, and gushing forth into streams of affection for his fellow-men. The grace of Christ, the sanctifying influences of the Holy Spirit, and the necessity of faith evidenced by a holy life, were his constant themes in public and in private. He would sometimes become so earnest, that, forgetting his manuscript, he would lean over the pulpit, and with his lion-like eye fixed upon some attentive hearer in the congregation, he would seem as if he was reading the very thoughts of the sinner's heart, and arraigning him before God for the murder of the soul. He was fond of preaching. He felt that it was an honourable employment, and never declined when asked, unless for some cogent reason, which every one would appreciate when named.

"But it was not in his pulpit ministrations only that he sought opportunity to preach Christ. Whenever we stopped at night, during a tour of several hundred miles, and sought lodging in the log-cabin of the pioneer settlers, he never failed, either in the evening or morning, to call the members of the family, as well as the sojourners present, around the domestic altar, to read a portion of God's word, comment on it, and then invite all to unite with him in prayer. In this way he not only inspired respect for religion, but also for its teachers.

"I remember very distinctly one of these occasions. He was making a running commentary on Romans viii., and had begun to remark on the 3rd verse, when a young woman present interposed a question, which implied that the law of God was defective, and needed to be annulled or set aside, because of its imperfection. He seemed to be aroused as if by an electric shock, and turning round towards the questioner, he said in his own peculiar manner, 'Don't you hear the Apostle say that the law was *weak through the flesh ?'* And then he proceeded to descant in a most lucid manner, and with thrilling effect on his hearers, upon the holiness, justice, and goodness of the law,—showing that it was honourable to God and just to man, and for that very reason rendered the exercise of mercy through Christ glorious to God.

"Naturally of a quick and excitable temperament, he felt very keenly an unprovoked injury or wrong. At the same time, I have met with few men who, I think, were possessed of a more ready disposition to forgive an offender than he was, upon a proper manifestation of repentance. For two years successively he accompanied me in my visitation of the diocese, relieving me of much of the duty of reading prayers and preaching. In every place the people manifested an eager desire to hear him. To this day they retain a very pleasing remembrance of his labours, and the announcement of his death will draw forth many a deep sigh from hundreds who cherish a grateful recol-

52　　CONNEXION WITH LOUISVILLE.

lection of his labours for their spiritual and eternal good.

"I am sorry, my dear Sir, that the time to which I am limited does not allow me to seek for many more gratifying reminiscences which I am sure exist, of one who by his Christian spirit and burning zeal in the cause of our blessed Redeemer, endeared himself to every Churchman in America who enjoyed the pleasure of his acquaintance. Would that the mantle of his faith, charity, and zeal, might rest upon us all!

　　　　　　　　　　"I remain

　　　　　"Your affectionate and faithful brother,

　　　　　　　　　　　"JAMES H. OTEY,

　　　　　　　　　　　　Bishop of Tennessee.

"To the Rev. H. Caswell, D. D., &c."

The event last mentioned by Mrs. Wheat obliged Mr. and Mrs. Leacock to leave Tennessee, and they soon afterwards went to the warm welcome of their friends in Louisville, Kentucky, under the following circumstances. At Louisville, Dr. Cook was now settled, together with the Harts, the Andersons, and other families once connected with St. Paul's at Lexington. These old acquaintances earnestly desired Mr. Leacock to become again their pastor, and to undertake the laborious task of "building up" a small congregation, worshipping in an old and unseemly church. This church had been almost deserted in consequence of the erection of a new and handsome edifice by the people under the charge of the Rev. W. Jackson. Mr. Anderson, aware of the power of Mr. Leacock, and believing that he could persuade him to throw himself into the breach, went two hundred miles by the stage-coach to Franklin, and determined to take no refusal. He seized Mr. Leacock with friendly violence, and actually brought him back with him to Louisville. Mr. Leacock commenced in that City with a kind of forlorn hope, and after some weeks returned to Franklin for his family.

Louisville then contained nearly forty thousand inhabitants, and has probably more than doubled that population at the present time. Its situation on the Ohio river renders it a most important commercial emporium, while railroads connecting it with the interior of Kentucky bring the produce of that fertile country on board the numerous steamers which perpetually crowd the landing-place. The people, though excitable, are hospitable, warm-hearted, and intelligent. Mr. Leacock already possessed many influential friends among them, and it is probable that if he had decided on a permanent engagement with them, he would have found a wide sphere of usefulness. A handsome stipend was promised to him, but he had determined that his stay should be but brief, and that he would never again live under the jurisdiction of the ecclesiastical authority of Kentucky.

For six months, however, he laboured most successfully in augmenting the congregation and in giving the people time, confidence, and opportunity to obtain a permanent minister. The Rev. Dr. Craik, of Louisville, thus writes respecting his ministrations at this period: "As a preacher, he was fervent, animated, and always interesting. Sometimes he produced a most startling sensation. Once, referring to the many good and able men who have been the propagators of false doctrine, he said, 'Do you suppose that the devil does not know how to choose his agents?' Another time, 'Do you know who was the first Unitarian? It was the devil.' 'If thou be the Son of God, &c.*'"

Mrs. Jackson, widow of the clergyman mentioned on the last page, states that Mr. Leacock's intercourse with her husband was of the most fraternal and agreeable character. She adds, "I remember that he was particularly forcible in his sermons on the doctrine of the Trinity, and though he was in the habit of introducing the most pointed remarks on that subject, the Unitarians went much to hear him, and had a great respect for his character."

Another lady, Mrs. Field, says, "During his short residence in Louisville he endeared himself to his people by the warmth of his own affections. His visits were like a gleam of sunshine to the sorrowful and the suffering. He seemed to live a life of childlike faith, never doubting his Father's love, ever looking to Him for strength. Once he preached a very solemn sermon on the certain punishment of the wicked. It was evident that the listeners were almost spell-bound. I said, 'Your sermon produced a great impression.' He looked quite sad, and answered, 'Yes, fear stirs up men's souls, but how few hearts would have been

---

* Matt. iv. 6.

melted by the story of the Saviour's dying love!' In his visits from house to house he often made stirring appeals to those who stood aloof from the body of Christ. When he found that a heart was touched, he would say, 'Now, my brother, let us kneel down and pray together.' A person very dear to him once said in his presence, 'I wish I had never been born.' He seemed much affected, and replied, 'What, when you know that Christ died for you?' His constant theme was the Divine love manifested in Christ Jesus. He became so dear to us, that to part from him was a great sorrow."

In April, 1840, I revisited Kentucky from Canada, and after a journey of about nine hundred miles, found myself among my former associates at Louisville. I shall never forget the hearty welcome which I received from Mr. and Mrs. Leacock, and from the principal persons of their congregation. Dr. Cooke stated that Mr. Leacock was producing a powerful effect in the place, being distinguished by the boldness and decision with which he gave utterance to unpopular and unpalatable truths. Instead of being offended with his plainness, the people had the good sense to perceive the practical worth of such a preacher. They respected him for his sincerity, and would have made great sacrifices to retain him among them as a regular pastor.

Since the general dispersion of his friends at Lexington, he had never felt at home in the West, and had preferred to act only as a missionary. There were no local ties as yet to bind him to any part of the United States, in which he always felt himself in some sense a foreigner. There can be no doubt also that change of place was not wholly unsuited to his character and habits. Wherever he dwelt he was strongly impressed with the conviction that in this life he had no abiding place, and that his only true home was in that Jerusalem which *hath* foundations, whose builder and maker is God.

A Committee of the House of Bishops in the American General Convention of 1856, made some valuable observations on the best mode of employing the various gifts bestowed on men for the edifying of the Church. "There are men," they state, " whose temperaments incline them to be constantly moving from place to place. Connected with this constitutional peculiarity, there is generally a frankness and cordiality of manner which renders such persons favourites wherever they go. They may not possess any great breadth or variety of learning, nor any great powers of thought; but they have a faculty of correct and close observation, a knowledge of men as individuals and in masses, and perhaps extraordinary skill and tact in controlling them. In this class will be found those best calculated of all, perhaps, in the Church, to fill the office of evangelists. Such a corps of active labourers seems almost indispensable to the complete organization of the Church according to the primitive model."

Mr. Leacock's circumstances had been, as before mentioned, considerably straitened while in Franklin, and the idea had occurred to him that he might, by the purchase of a farm, secure a competence for his family in the event of his decease. His health was now much impaired, and he wished to obtain a situation in which he might rest himself and recruit his energies. He desired also to enjoy facilities for ready communication with his aged father in Barbados.

Accordingly, with the remnant of his means, he had already purchased a small estate near the seashore, and not far from the town of New Brunswick, in New Jersey. His friends in Kentucky greatly disapproved of this step, and assured him that he could never succeed as an agriculturist; but their solicitations and representations were alike fruitless, and he remained in Louisville only to complete his six months as a wayfaring man and a sojourner. The work of God, however, prospered in his hand, and under his successors. The congregation, of which he undertook the charge in its day of weakness, has been steadily improving and enlarging itself to the present day. The capacity of the church has been several times increased for the accommodation of the worshippers. Two new parish churches have also been erected since Mr. Leacock's brief incumbency, and a third is now in progress.

A letter from Mrs. Leacock, written soon after my visit to Louisville in 1840, showed that the persevering efforts of the congregation to retain her husband had proved fruitless. " We live," she wrote, " with our kind friends, the Harts, where it is likely we shall remain so long as we stay in Louisville. This is a sore subject to the ears of our congregation (I mean our leaving Louisville for New Jersey), but Mr. Leacock says he sees no alternative, and that go we must in July." Accordingly in July they proceeded to their destination, and shortly afterwards Mr. Leacock appeared in his new character of a New Jersey farmer.

He did not, however, permit agricultural labours to divert his attention from the great work of his ministry. In the autumn of this year he visited Connecticut, where he preached a striking sermon at an ordination held by the bishop of the diocese in the town of Bridgeport. For a few Sundays he continued to officiate in that neighbourhood, but his anchorage in New Jersey compelled him to return, and to confine his ministrations to places in the vicinity of his new home. During the winter he supplied the pulpit of Christ-Church, New Brunswick, the rector being temporarily absent.

In 1841 he spent some time in the West Indies, endeavouring to recover the property of which he had been deprived, and to which his son would be entitled in right of his mother. In this endeavour he was partially successful. Soon after his return to America, I accidentally met him in Broadway during the session of the General Convention in New York. He was rejoiced to see an old Kentucky friend, and gave me much interesting information respecting his plans and prospects.

About this time he was visited at his farm by the Rev. Mr. Pitkin, who had succeeded him at Louis-

SETTLEMENT AT PERTH AMBOY.

ville. Mr. Pitkin had heard so many things reported in his praise, that he longed to form his acquaintance, and went on a kind of pilgrimage to visit him in his rural retreat, eight hundred miles eastward of Kentucky. He found him at work in his barn, and met with a most cordial reception. The two clergymen sat down on the hay, and long remained together in agreeable and Christian conversation. " I sat there as long as possible," says Mr. Pitkin, " drinking in his sweet speech, and learning how he had held hearts so knit to him. I left him at last, but shall never forget him. He being dead, yet speaketh to us by the noble example of his self-sacrifice."

Shortly after his return from the West Indies, he was desired by Bishop Doane to undertake the charge of two little stations, one *five* and the other *twelve* miles distant from his residence. At these places he laboured faithfully and zealously until 1843, when he was prevailed upon to part with his farm, and to become rector of St. Peter's, in Perth Amboy. The situation of Perth Amboy is pleasant and healthy. It stands on a neck of land at the head of Raritan river, on the great thoroughfare between New York and Philadelphia. At a very early period in American history it carried on a trade with the West Indies, having one of the best harbours on the continent. The church in this place is of a comparatively ancient date, having been founded in the times anterior to the Revolution.

Mr. Leacock, as usual, soon made friends in his new parish, and being pleased with the situation became apparently settled for life. During four years he continued in Perth Amboy, and fully maintained his already high reputation as a faithful minister of the word of God.

In the summer of 1843, he had the great pleasure of receiving another of his old Kentucky friends. Dr. Coit visited him from New Rochelle, and wrote to me as follows on the 29th of July. "I had a spare Sunday a short time since, and ran down to Perth Amboy to spend it with Hamble Leacock. He is well, and very comfortably situated, and took great delight in talking over old Kentucky times."

In 1847, the decaying health of his father, and the necessity of looking after the property of his son (now of age), obliged him to revisit his native island of Barbados. He left his parish at Perth Amboy in the charge of a clerical friend, and received the following letter from Bishop Doane to Bishop Parry, the successor of Bishop Coleridge:

"To the Right Reverend the Lord Bishop of Barbados.

"This is to commend the Reverend Hamble James Leacock, a Presbyter of this diocese, who is about to visit some of the islands of your Lordship's diocese, as a brother, faithful and beloved, and worthy of all confidence and kindness.

"Affectionately in the bonds of Jesus Christ,
"G. W. DOANE.
"Riverside, Easter Monday, 1847."

Mr. Leacock expected to return to his duties at

Perth Amboy in the spring of 1848. Being, however, detained longer than he had anticipated, he was informed that his parishioners were somewhat impatiently awaiting his return. He immediately sent over his resignation of the rectorship, and terminated his connexion with the diocese of New Jersey. All attempts to induce him to reconsider this decision were fruitless, and in 1849, having settled all his affairs in the United States, he appeared once more as a West Indian clergyman.

CHAPTER IV.

Reasons for his Return. State of Nevis. African practices. Obeah. Mr. Leacock delivers Lectures against Obeah. Death of the Obeah-man. Effect of Charms on the African. Return to Barbados. Temporary Charge of St. Peter's. Death of Amos Cleaver and Dr. Cooke. Mr. Leacock is appointed to the Chapel at Bridgetown. Testimonial of the Parishioners of St. Peter's. Commencement of efforts in behalf of Africa. Formation of the Society for the furtherance of the Gospel. Outbreak of Cholera. Death of Mrs. Leacock.

It was not a mere fondness for change, and still less was it the communication from Perth Amboy, which induced Mr. Leacock to attach himself again to the West Indies. His father was now very aged, and indeed died in the following year, after a long and gradual decline. His only daughter, Elizabeth, was about this time married, and happily settled in Barbados. The apprenticeship system from which he had justly apprehended evil consequences, had been found inexpedient on trial, and had given way to the complete abolition of negro slavery on the 1st of August, 1838. The relative position of blacks and whites was now fully understood, and, although West Indian property had in many instances become nearly valueless, it was clear to Mr. Leacock that the two races might now *exist together* in harmony. He found that old preju-

STATE OF THINGS IN NEVIS. 63

dices originating in slavery had in a great measure
died away, and the people of Barbados, who had all
but ejected him in 1827, gave him a cordial and respectful greeting twenty years afterwards. While engaged on his son's business in that island he performed
for several months the duties of minister of his native
parish, during the illness of the rector, to the edifica-
tion and delight of the congregation.

Having concluded this brief engagement he revisited Nevis, where he found a strong affection still
subsisting towards him among his old parishioners.
When he spoke of the possibility of his returning
to the United States, many of them implored him
with tears to become once more their pastor. He
yielded to their entreaties, and after definitely resign-
ing the charge of the parish of Perth Amboy, again
occupied his former position in the church at Charlestown.

But twelve or thirteen years had made great
changes among the people. Many old friends of the
pastor were dead, and others had departed. The negroes had too generally become idle since the acqui-
sition of liberty, and with idleness had betaken themselves to the bad habits of former times. African
superstitions had been re-introduced by a number of
re-captured slaves, and the horrid practice of Obeah,
as it is called, was spreading terror throughout the
island.

Mr. Leacock, being a man of known energy and
courage, was armed by the governor with the authority of a magistrate, and exerted himself in appre-
hending and punishing some of the worst criminals.

64 AFRICAN PRACTICES—OBEAH.

But there was an Obeah man whose influence had become so extraordinary that he had managed to paralyze even the strong hand of justice. He was believed to possess a certain charm, by which he could at any time cause the death of those who fell under his curse. He was in reality a most accomplished poisoner. He could insinuate the means of destruction into vegetables, melons, and other fruits as they grew in the field or in the garden. Through the agency of his creatures presents were conveyed to his enemies which occasioned their speedy death. At length no one dared to receive a gift of any article of food. So deep was the cunning of the "doctor," as he was called, that hitherto it had been impossible to bring legal evidence to bear upon him. Besides this, few could be found who possessed the courage to come forward as witnesses against him, or to find him guilty if brought before a jury.

Under these circumstances, Mr. Leacock announced his intention of delivering a course of public lectures exposing the infamous practice of Obeah. The Obeah-man, on the contrary, declared that if Mr. Leacock should persist in this intention, a curse should rest upon him and that he would certainly die. Nothing daunted, the intrepid pastor proceeded with his lectures, though many of his congregation already regarded him as a dead man. Meantime the "doctor" was engaged in the preparation of the most deadly poisons to secure the fulfilment of his curse. It is supposed that he incautiously tasted some of these in order to assure himself of their potency. Certain it is that his corpse was found among some sugar-canes, frightfully disfigured, yet without any visible cause of death.

To show the terrible effect of a curse upon the mind and body of the African, Mr. Leacock related to me the following circumstance as having happened within his own knowledge. Three negro men having stolen a pig from a woman of their own race, were solemnly cursed by her. In their terror they restored the pig, but the woman refused to revoke the curse. She buried a piece of the animal in the ground, and assured the thieves that before it should decay they would all undoubtedly perish. In a short time the three men began to grow weak and became unable to perform their accustomed work. Their employer went to the woman and entreated her to remove the imprecation. She apparently consented, and seemed to make light of the whole transaction. But nothing could re-assure the three victims, who gradually pined away, and not long afterwards died.

In 1852 Mr. Leacock returned to Barbados, where in July he took charge of the parish of St. Peter's, Speightstown, in the absence of the Rev. W. Payne, the rector, and retained it to the end of 1853. In the autumn of that year, being resident in England, I was sent with others on a deputation to the Episcopal Board of Missions, which assembled in October, at New-York, during the session of the General Convention. On this occasion I had the pleasure of meeting Mr. Leacock's brother, the Rev. Dr. Leacock, of New Orleans, who attended the Convention as a clerical deputy from the diocese of Louisiana. I met also Mr. Hamble Leacock's only son, Benjamin, a prom-

ising young clergyman of the American Church, who
had recently received Holy Orders after completing
his studies at the Episcopal Theological Seminary of
Virginia. At the same time I heard of the death of
Mr. Cleaver, who had fallen a victim to his fidelity
to his parishioners in Mississippi during the prevalence of yellow fever. It was during this session of
the Convention that Dr. Cooke was removed to another life, having attained to the age of seventy-one.
A last notice of this remarkable man, as a friend to
Mr. Leacock, will hardly be inappropriate in this
place.

In 1844 Dr. Cooke resigned his medical professor-
ship and retired to Woodlawn, a beautiful farm in
the neighbourhood of Louisville. A few years later,
in 1848, he purchased a large unimproved estate on
the southern bank of the Ohio, about thirty miles
above Louisville, where his energies were employed
in the labours of the farmer and the pioneer. The
wild beauties of nature, which he intensely enjoyed,
the love of his family and the consolations of religion,
were here his solace and delight. His biographer
says that it was deeply affecting to see that strong old
man weeping at bidding adieu to the Christian minister who from time to time celebrated, at his secluded
home on the Ohio, the solemn offices of the Church.

For many years he had been subject upon exposure, to violent attacks of inflammation of the lungs.
These he had often removed by the prompt application of his own vigorous treatment. The attacks became so frequent under the exposure incident to his
new mode of life on the Ohio, that his strong consti-

tution gave way, and, on the 19th of October, 1853, he breathed his last, with a firm trust in the mercy of the Saviour, whom he had loved and served for the greater part of a long life. While on his death-bed, for many weeks, and until within a few hours of his death, the Greek Testament was his constant companion. All day long, and every day, he pored over its sacred pages with critical attention and devout affection. His mind retained its power and freshness to the last. Truth and love he found embodied in the Word of the Almighty, and on that his soul rested, in life and death, with satisfied delight.

While his old friends in America were thus going the way of all the earth, Mr. Leacock was putting forth all his energies in Barbados, and becoming an influential clergyman of the diocese under Bishop Parry. In December, 1853, Mr. Paine returning from England, Mr. Leacock resigned into his hands the charge of the parish of St. Peter's. The following account of the proceedings on this occasion is taken from the "Barbadian" newspaper of December 14th:—

" TESTIMONIAL TO MR. LEACOCK.

"We have great satisfaction in placing on our page the following handsome address of the parishioners of St. Peter to the Rev. Hamble J. Leacock, with the reverend gentleman's grateful reply. This is the second instance which we have had the pleasure of recording in our journal, within the last six years, of the good feeling of the parishioners of St. Peter on the subject of pastoral superintendence, and

68   TESTIMONIAL TO MR. LEACOCK.

their just appreciation of the labours of faithful and
zealous ministers, who have happened temporarily to
perform the responsible duties of parish priest in the
absence of the rector—viz.: the Rev. H. R. Redwar
in 1847, and the Rev. H. J. Leacock, for the last
seventeen months. The separation which is now
about to take place, we can well imagine will be
painful to both parties.

" The reverend gentleman, who is the subject of
the following correspondence, has evinced a generous
and disinterested feeling in intimating his intention
to appropriate the greater part of the munificent gift
of the parishioners to the endowment of a ' Coleridge
Scholarship ' at Codrington College. We are authorized, however, to state, that it was the unanimous
wish of the donors that the whole sum should be laid
out in the purchase of a piece of plate, and that Mr.
Leacock has yielded to their wish.

" The deputation of the parishioners waited upon
the reverend gentleman at the rectory.

" ' Reverend and dear Sir,
" ' As parishioners of Saint Peter, and especially
as members of the congregation of the parish church,
we are unwilling that you should relinquish the trust
which has devolved upon you during the temporary
absence of our rector in England, without conveying
to you the strong sense we entertain of the faithful
and efficient manner in which you have discharged
your ministerial responsibilities.

" ' Your earnest and impressive teaching of the

truths of the Gospel, the zeal manifested in your unwearied efforts to promote the spiritual welfare of the people, and your diligent attention to other pastoral relations which exist between the minister and his flock, have endeared you to us, and call for an expression of our gratitude and affectionate regard. In offering, on the eve of our separation, this our testimony to your worth, we desire also to present you with a somewhat more substantial, but inadequate mark of our esteem, and beg your acceptance of this purse, containing the sum of three hundred and fifty dollars, which we request you will appropriate to the purchase of a piece of plate, to perpetuate the remembrance of the connexion which has so happily subsisted between us for the last seventeen months.

" ' With our sincere wishes that your ministry may be continued to the Church of this island, and that God may in all things bless your labours and devotion to his service,

" ' We remain, reverend and dear Sir,

" ' In behalf of the parishioners of St. Peter,

and your late congregation,

" ' Yours sincerely,

" ' Sir R. A. Alleyne, Bart., Francis Goding, N. Foderingham, Jones Pile (Members of H. M. Council), Wm. H. Farnum, James D. Bend, Isaac Skinner, Benjamin Norville, J. C. B. Scantlebury, John D. Emptage, G. R. Challenor, William Jordan, Robert Challenor.

" ' The Rev. Hamble J. Leacock.' "

" ' Gentlemen of the Deputation,

" ' I cannot decline this honourable testimony which you, and certain parishioners, and especially the congregation of your parish church, have offered me; and at once I beg to thank you, and to appoint you as the organ through which my grateful acknowledgments may be conveyed to every individual.

" ' As an expression of thankfulness for my labours during my short residence amongst you, nothing can be more satisfactory to me than your address, since it induces a hope that *my labours have not been in vain.* But the very circumstance of a general approval, which so augments my sense of obligation, creates in me an anxious fear, lest, in the discharge of my ministerial duties, I may be found to have been unfaithful. You have indeed strongly testified to my earnestness and diligence in endeavouring to promote the spiritual welfare of my charge; but, gentlemen, I know somewhat of the magnitude of ministerial responsibility; and the consciousness of my own inefficiency, humbles me under the conviction that I am utterly unworthy of the favourable opinion so honestly entertained by you.

" ' You have honoured me with another evidence of your favourable regard,—an evidence more weighty indeed, but not more acceptable than the one to which I have already alluded. This purse of gold,—this free-will offering of a generous, magnanimous people, shall, *with their concurrence,* be consecrated to the service of our common Lord and Master,—at least the greater portion of it. It is my desire to offer it

APPOINTMENT TO ST. LEONARD'S.

as a contribution towards 'The Coleridge Scholarship,' to be established in Codrington College,—there to perpetuate the memory of our connexion and reciprocal attachment; and to afford me the additional satisfaction of anticipating the day in which it will be returned to you all, in abundant showers of the Divine blessing. *One of your own sons*, educated through that very Scholarship, and moulded and fashioned by the grace of God, may be sent to the inhabitants of this parish, as Paul was to the Gentiles,—' a minister and a witness, ... to open their eyes, to turn them from darkness to light, and from the power of Satan unto God, that they may receive forgiveness of sins, and inheritance among them which are sanctified by faith in Christ's name.'

" ' With the balance of your liberal present, I will purchase a piece of plate, merely to tell my children's children that their grandsire received from his countrymen, after fifty-nine suns had rolled o'er his head, the honourable testimony which renders this day one of the brightest and most distinguished of his humble life.

" ' That the Divine blessing may be ever with you all, to keep you in the ways of holiness, and peace, and usefulness, is the prayer of

" 'Gentlemen,

" ' Your faithful friend and servant,

" ' H. J. LEACOCK.

" ' Monday, Dec. 12th, 1853.' "

In January, 1854, Mr. Leacock was appointed to the charge of the chapel of ease of St. Leonard's in

EFFORTS IN BEHALF OF AFRICA.

Bridgetown. But at this time a cause was gaining ground in the West Indies, which, in process of time, enlisted his entire bodily and mental powers, and led him on to the attainment of the high honour of dying for Christ, the Master whom he had so long and so faithfully served.

The debased condition of Western Africa had long furnished matter of melancholy reflection to Christian philanthropists. The idea had been suggested that the work of the missions to that country called loudly for the co-operation of the inhabitants of the West Indies, partly on the ground of natural relationship, and partly as a debt of common justice. It was also supposed that from these colonies might be obtained missionaries who were not only accustomed to a tropical sun, but who, by reason of African descent, might encounter, with less danger than Europeans, the risks of an African climate. Codrington College had been originally founded, as we have seen, for the education of missionaries, and was made dependent for its support on labour derived originally from Africa.

Early in 1847, a change in Codrington College placed at its head the Rev. R. Rawle, late Fellow of Trinity College, Cambridge, who, from the first, evinced a peculiar interest in Africa, with a strong sense of its claims upon the College. In the following year Barbados received for its Governor, in the person of Sir William Colebrooke, an individual to whom Africa had long been an object of especial concern. Throughout the whole community, too,

FORMATION OF A SOCIETY. 73

from various causes, a lively feeling had been excited respecting that unhappy continent.

At this juncture, the publication by Mr. Rawle of extracts from a parliamentary report, placed in his hands by Sir William Colebrooke, served to show the existence of an encouraging opening for Christian instruction among the natives of Africa, and it was consequently agreed to bring the matter before the public through the medium of the Barbados Church Society. Accordingly, a meeting of that society was convened by Bishop Parry on the 15th of November, 1850, at which resolutions were passed to the effect "that a mission to Western Africa would be a work peculiarly suitable to the Church in the West Indies, where the population consists so largely of persons deriving their origin from that country,—that the time for such an enterprise had arrived,—and that it would especially become Barbados to be forward in this great and good work," inviting at the same time the co-operation of the whole West Indian Church. On the 16th of June, 1851, the Jubilee day of the Society for Propagating the Gospel, it was determined to make the African Mission the object of a distinct society, to be called "The West Indian Church Association for the Furtherance of the Gospel in Western Africa." It was proposed to direct the efforts of this society to parts of Africa unoccupied by the older missions either of the English or of the American Church.

The society, thus founded, received the cordial approval of the West Indian and English Bishops, the

4

74 FORMATION OF A SOCIETY.

Society for Propagating the Gospel, and many of the governors of the West Indian Islands. The British Government was also pleased to regard the undertaking with favour, and the Secretary of State, on the 24th of February, 1851, promised to give it whatever countenance and protection could be legitimately afforded.

Contributions now began to flow into the treasury of the Society. The Society for Propagating the Gospel gave 1000*l.* from its Jubilee Fund. Collections were made in Barbados and other islands, and missionary meetings were attempted with satisfactory results. The widow and sons of the late well-known philanthropist, Sir T. F. Buxton, remitted the sum of 135*l.*, and a Committee organized for the purpose in the University of Cambridge obtained in a few days contributions to the amount of 158*l.*

Encouraged by the amount of sympathy and aid already received, the Society determined to commence work in Africa as soon as practicable. Bishop Parry therefore, as President of the Board, opened a direct communication with Dr. Vidal, the first Bishop of Sierra Leone, and received from him two letters conveying assurances of his interest in the projected mission, as well as valuable advice in regard to the part of Western Africa in which it should be commenced. As yet, however, no man could be found willing or ready to undertake the certain difficulties and risks which such a mission involved.

Mr. Leacock was one of those who from the first had taken a lively interest in the design. Sometimes

indeed he expressed to Mrs. Leacock his earnest wish
to be sent on such a mission himself. She trembled
at the thought of so perilous an enterprise, and assured him that if sent to Africa he could not, at his
time of life, withstand the malaria of that pestilential
climate. He did his best, however, to promote the
objects of the mission within his sphere, and in the
district of St. Peter's the collections at his missionary
meetings, in nine months, amounted to more than
twenty-six pounds. The Bishop, in recommending
this example to his clergy generally, remarked that
" such meetings might add to the labours of the clergy,
but the benefits arising from them would be largely
shared by the people themselves, and the piety of the
country would gain strength and maturity." In fact,
the advantages, direct and indirect, of such meetings
are too well known in England to admit of any reasonable doubt.

In January, 1854 (as I have stated), Mr. Leacock
was appointed by the Bishop to the charge of the
chapel of ease of St. Leonard's in Bridgetown. In
the spring of the same year the cholera broke out in
the island with fearful destructiveness, and at one
time more than twenty dead bodies lay unburied in
Mr. Leacock's churchyard. Owing to the general
terror it was impossible to hire labourers to dig the
graves, and Mr. Leacock found himself compelled to
apply to the authorities for bands of soldiers and prisoners to aid him in that necessary work. Although
Mrs. Leacock had a strong presentiment that her end
was at hand, she shared her husband's unremitting

exertions in attending upon the sick and dying, without distinction of party, sect, character, or colour. At length, in the month of August, when the disease seemed to have nearly spent its strength, this admirable woman was struck down, and after a period of unspeakable agony, endured with Christian fortitude, breathed her last. Her grave is still tended with watchful affection by the hands of those who loved her while living, and who reverence her memory when dead.

CHAPTER V.

Mr. Leacock volunteers to go as a Missionary to Africa. He is accepted, and is joined by Duport. His Negro Servant desires to accompany him. Letter to Archdeacon Trew. Arrival in London. He attends a Meeting of the Church Emigrants' Aid Society. He visits the Crystal Palace. Visit to Wiltshire—Stonehenge—Salisbury. Meeting of the S. P. G. His Cheerfulness. Conversation with Young Persons. His views of Prophecy, of the Church of Rome, and of the Church of England. His opinion of the Voluntary System. Thankfulness for Mercies. Note on the Effects of Emancipation in the West Indies.

FOR some time Mr. Leacock continued crushed and almost stupefied by the terrible blow which had fallen upon him, and even the thought of Africa seemed to have lost its interest. At length, after the lapse of half a year, the idea of volunteering to lead the projected mission flashed suddenly upon his mind. On the 19th of March, 1855, being then over sixty years of age, he offered himself to his bishop in a letter containing the following characteristic sentences :

"The Church calls, and some one must answer. But few years' service are now before me. I rise therefore to save my brethren in the ministry, the young who are the hope of the Church, the old who are the stay of large families. Believe me, I do not

78 HIS OFFER IS ACCEPTED.

suppose that my services, unaided by Divine grace, can accomplish any thing. To God alone must we look for any strength, or for any success, whatever may be the character of the instrument employed, whether young or old, learned or unlearned. If the Board concur with your lordship I will go; but 'I will go in the strength of the Lord God; and make mention of his righteousness, and of his only.' My lord, in placing my services at your disposal, I have done only *my duty*, and I shall be satisfied with the issue, be it what it may."

It was with deep regret that Mr. Leacock's family learned of his determination to venture on this mission. He seemed, however, so earnest in the cause, and so zealous for the glory of God and the good of souls, that they did not attempt to resist his purpose. The bishop, of course, did not feel himself at liberty to discourage the offer, nor the Mission Board to refuse it. It was accordingly brought before a special meeting of the association held at Bridgetown, Sir William Colebrooke presiding, on the 16th of May. The offer was unanimously accepted, though not without many painful feelings at the loss of an individual so generally esteemed and beloved, and as a clergyman so valuable to the diocese. On this occasion Mr. Leacock acknowledged his election in a very feeling speech, from the report of which, printed in the " Barbadian," the following is an extract :—

" It is through the grace of the Son of God that I have not shrunk from engaging in the work; and I humbly trust, through the same grace, to hold *on*, and to hold *out*, till a more youthful, enterprising, and efficient champion of the Cross be found to take my place. And, if the example of an old soldier of the Cross can fire with true missionary spirit and Christian zeal the bosoms of some noble, brave, disinterested, accomplished youth, of our little island, and cause them to rise up, and quit the soft, smooth, downy, attractive elegances of polished life, and prepare and arm them for that rugged, perilous warfare, and to follow me in it, I shall then know that I have not lived in vain, that I have not spent my strength for nought. With hand and heart will I receive them, cheerfully give place to them, or remain and labour with them, as ye shall see best. And when my work is done, I will thankfully go to bed in Afric's dust, and sweetly and quietly rest from the toil and burden and heat of the day, till the bright morning dawn, in which the trumpet shall announce the approach of our great King, and we shall rise up, and mount up to meet Him in the air, and be with Him for ever."

A young black man, of good character, Mr. John H. A. Duport, readily accepted an invitation to accompany Mr. Leacock as an industrial help in the work of civilization, as well as a subordinate teacher for missionary objects. Mr. Duport had been educated at the Mission House attached to Codrington College. He had been well instructed in the Holy Scriptures, history, geography, mathematics, and arithmetic, besides which he had formed some acquaintance with Latin, and was a good practical mechanic.

Mr. Leacock now disposed of his worldly goods,

80 HIS SERVANT WISHES TO GO WITH HIM.

in the full expectation of never seeing his native land again. To the very last his old negro female servant continued earnestly imploring him to allow her to bear him company. "Oh, massa," she said, "who will take care of you in Africa, who will nurse you when you are sick, who will attend on you? Oh, take me with you, dear massa, take me with you to Africa." But Mr. Leacock would not permit this faithful creature to share his perils, and, to her bitter grief, she was left with her friends in Barbados.

Archdeacon Trew of the Bahamas had been deeply interested in the projected mission, and had furnished Mr. Leacock with an introductory letter to his friend, Governor Hill of Sierra Leone. Mr. Leacock wrote to the archdeacon the following letter on the eve of his departure :—

"Bridgetown, Barbados, July 13, 1855.

"Dear Mr. Archdeacon,

'I cannot leave the West Indies without acknowledging the receipt of your letter, forwarded by the Rev. T. Clarke. It was very considerate and very kind in you to think of your African missionary at the moment of his departure for the scene of his future labours, and the more so because he is a stranger to you. The letter to Governor Hill is a valuable appendage to my little parcel, and I hope I shall have the pleasure of seeing his Excellency and presenting it myself.

"I thank you, Rev. and dear Sir, for your warm-hearted wishes for my success, and also for your promise of assistance. A man who can feel and act

LETTER TO ARCHDEACON TREW.　81

as you do will never fail to pray for a blessing on the
labours of God's servants. I need not, therefore, beg
you to remember me in your prayers. It will be a
comfort and an encouragement in my journeyings,
labours, and solicitude, to *know* that, in the Bahamas,
as well as in this little island, I have Christian friends
who sympathize with me, who feel as deeply interested in my work as I do myself, and who will often
be found with me at the throne of grace, begging for
that help which alone can keep me from the evil of
the world, strengthen me for my work, and crown my
labours with that success which shall make our hearts
'rejoice in the God of our salvation.' I have nothing
to declare but '*Jesus Christ and Him crucified*,' pardon through his blood, justification through his righteousness, sanctification by his Spirit; I know nothing
else, and I am determined to know nothing else. This
will I teach, and trust in God to give it his blessing.

"I am very busy getting ready for the steamer
which is expected this evening, so I must lay by this.
As soon as I can get fairly into my work, and have
somewhat to write about, you shall hear from me.
May the Lord bless you and your labours, and preserve many years your valuable life for the good of
his Church.

"Yours very sincerely and faithfully," &c.

The chapelry in Bridgetown having been provided
for, Mr. Leacock and his companion embarked on the
15th of July on board the steamer for England, there
being no direct communication between the West

Indies and the African coast. Many tears were shed
on this occasion, recalling to mind the departure of
St. Paul from Miletus, when the Ephesian elders
" wept sore, and fell on Paul's neck, and kissed him,
sorrowing most for the words which he spake, that
they should see his face no more." Like St. Paul,
the veteran missionary might have said to his mourning friends, " Remember that by the space of three years
I ceased not to warn every one night and day with
tears; and how I kept back nothing that was profitable to you, but have showed you, and have taught
you publicly, and from house to house. And now, behold, I go bound in the spirit, not knowing the things
that shall befall me. But none of these things move
me, neither count I my life dear unto myself, so that
I might finish my course with joy, and the ministry,
which I have received of the Lord Jesus, to testify
the gospel of the grace of God."

His native land soon sunk below the western
horizon. He lost sight of the island in which he had
gone through so many vicissitudes, and in which,
" through evil report and good report," he had constantly maintained the testimony of a good conscience in the sight of God. He beheld Barbados no
more.

While Mr. Leacock was on his voyage, the " Barbadian " newspaper reached his old parishioners in
Perth Amboy, informing them of the mission to which
he had devoted himself. The intelligence spread
itself among his American friends, and, on the

28th of July, Dr. Coit wrote me the following letter from his new parish at Troy (New York), enclosing the Barbados paper :—

"My dear Caswall,

" I received the enclosed paper a short time since from Perth Amboy, from some one of Hamble's old parishioners. It appears that he is going as a mis-sionary to Africa, and perhaps you can find out his residence and communicate with him. If so, bid him God speed from me, and tell him that if we never meet again in this world I shall never forget him, or cease to esteem and love him. I wrote to him two or three times, but perhaps my letters never reached him. How comes on Convocation, and how do you like your new Bishop ?

" Yours affectionately,
" T. W. Coit."

This was the first intimation I had received of the connexion of my old friend with the West African Mission. Immediately on receiving Dr. Coit's letter, I concluded that Mr. Leacock would proceed by way of England, and accordingly requested a friend in London to ascertain whether he had made his appear-ance in this country. The reply informed me that he had already been some time in London, at a lodg-ing in Cecil-street, in the Strand. I wrote to him on the 18th of August, and received the following an-swer :—

LETTER FROM LONDON.

London, August 28, 1855.

"My dear Caswall,

" Your warm-hearted salutation, ' *dear old friend*,' sounded in my ears like good news of a dear friend from a far country. I am in London, solitary in the midst of its millions, having found but two acquaintances, who reside so far from me that I seldom see them. The Bishop of Barbados is now in England, and the object of his visit *partly* and of mine *entirely*, is to make known as extensively as possible my mission and its design ; and to enlist in its favour, and receive the help of as many friends as it shall please God to make for me.

" In a few days I shall proceed to Bristol and Bath, where I expect some assistance ; but I must endeavour to find out your whereabouts, that so, if possible, I may once more look at you. I have no map of England at hand, and your letter is not sufficiently explanatory. But there is a difficulty. I am travelling at our Society's expense, and as your letter dated the 18th has only *now* reached me, I fear the expense of travelling. You will, I know, pardon this explanation, and not think me capable of a meanness. I am but the servant of a society. If the Society for the Propagation of the Gospel have a meeting near you, and I be required to attend it, it will be a good opportunity to see you. I shall leave England in October with the Bishop of Sierra Leone.

" Ben is not with me. He is in the ministry, and rector of a church in Mobile, Alabama, with a salary of three thousand dollars. He is a true man and a good son. Elizabeth is married and in comfortable circumstances. They are both dear children; notwithstanding I am alone and a wanderer, God only being with me.

"With affectionate remembrances to your dear wife and daughter, believe me," &c.

On the 27th of August I went to London, and on the next morning visited Mr. Leacock in Cecil-street. I found him in his lodging, sitting at a table, making out an account of his expenses, while Duport, an intelligent-looking black man, was working a problem in algebra. His hair had grown gray, but otherwise he was little changed since I had last seen him in 1841. Our meeting was extremely gratifying, and brought back a flood of old reminiscences. He mentioned, among other things, that he was at this time living on about eighteen pence a day, in order to avoid putting his society to any unnecessary expense. Instead of ordering a regular dinner, he was in the habit of purchasing a few simple eatables at a shop in the Strand.

On the following day he attended with me one of the preliminary meetings of the Anglo-American Church Emigrants' Aid Society. He was delighted to be informed that efforts were being made to retain in the fold of the Church the natives of Old England, who, to the number of about *fifty thousand* annually, take up their residence within the United States. He rejoiced in the formation of the society, not only on account of the spiritual advantages which it offered to the stranger in a strange land, but because he saw in it a method of fraternal intercourse and Christian co-operation between the Churches of England and America.

Mr. Leacock being a total stranger in England, I was anxious to show him some of the most interesting things connected with the metropolis. On the 31st I took him to the Crystal Palace, where we spent the greater part of the day. After wandering through the memorials of ancient nations, Assyria, Egypt, Greece, and Rome, after hearing some effective music, and examining choice and beautiful specimens of the vegetable world, we walked through the gardens, saw the geological models, and finally beheld a grand display of the fountains. As we returned, Mr. Leacock said that he had spent a day well worthy of remembrance. He assured me that the whole scene far exceeded any thing which he had expected to behold in this world. It served, he said, in a measure, to carry on his thoughts to the heavenly city, the New Jerusalem, having the glory of God, even like a jasper stone, clear as crystal. " And the building of the wall of it was of jasper: and the city was pure gold, like unto clear glass."

On the following day I took him home with me to Wiltshire, and, for the first time in his life, he rode on the top of a stage-coach. As we passed through the country, he expressed in the strongest terms his admiration of its beauty, and of the healthy appearance of the people. He assured me that he had always been a loyal British subject, like his ances-

tors before him, and that his allegiance had never
wavered.

On the 1st of September he preached in my
church at Figheldean, taking for his text the words,
" My son, give me thine heart." He showed that
God required mainly and principally the service of
the heart, and that we were bound to give Him not a
portion of our hearts, but the whole. The people
were deeply impressed by his earnest manner, as well
as by the thoughts to which he gave utterance. They
saw in him a man going forth with his life in his hand
for the sake of that religion which he preached.
Every word therefore took effect, and the discourse
will not soon be forgotten. In the evening he delivered a missionary address to a concourse of persons,
who completely filled the church, and who listened
to the speaker with admiration and delight.

On the following day I reminded him that England was formerly a heathen country like Africa, and
proposed to show him a vast idolatrous temple which
God's providence had preserved to the present time,
as if to remind us, in the midst of our boasted civilization, of the " rock whence we were hewn," and the
" hole of the pit from whence we were digged." Accordingly we walked about four miles across the open
plain, until we arrived at Stonehenge. The good missionary passed with me under the enormous overhang-
ing stones, and when we arrived at the broken altar,
near the centre, on which human victims are supposed
to have shed their blood, he viewed it with profound
emotion and awe. Through the surrounding colon-

MEETING AT SALISBURY.

nade he descried in the distance a small point like that of a needle rising above the horizon. On being told that this was the summit of Salisbury Cathedral, he spoke of Gospel times succeeding the dreary ages of idolatry, and expressed his firm belief that Africa, like England, would yet look heavenward, and stretch forth her hands unto God.

The next day was devoted to Salisbury, where we attended the Cathedral service, and partook of the Holy Communion, Archdeacon Grant preaching on the subject of Missions. The intoning of the service, being altogether new to Mr. Leacock, struck him rather painfully, and he could not at once bring himself to regard it as a natural mode of addressing supplications to the Almighty. In the evening we attended a large meeting held at the Council Chamber, in behalf of the Society for the Propagation of the Gospel. The bishop was in the chair, and among the speakers were Lord Nelson, Canon Bickersteth, Archdeacon Grant, and Canon White, of the diocese of Capetown. I was permitted to introduce Mr. Leacock to the assembly, and to make a brief statement respecting the mission in which he was engaged. Having been received in a warm-hearted manner, Mr. Leacock then rose and delivered an address full of pathos, in which he asked the sympathies of his English brethren, and described the wretched condition of the region to which he was proceeding. Every eye was fixed upon him, and when he ceased to speak it was evident that a decided impression had been created. Independently of the usual collection for the Society

for the Propagation of the Gospel, the kind-hearted
bishop set on foot a subscription for the West Indian
Mission, which immediately realized a considerable
sum.   From Salisbury Mr. Leacock returned to London, where he officiated for a few Sundays at the church
of St. Clement, in the Strand.

After his departure I wrote to the Bishop of Barbados, then in Malvern, and gave his Lordship a full
report of the meeting at Salisbury, and of the excellent effect produced by his good missionary.   The
bishop was much gratified, and replied that he felt it
as a matter for great thankfulness that his valued friend
and brother had met with so warm and cordial a reception.   He wrote to Mr. Leacock on the subject,
who addressed to me on the 11th, in reply to a letter
of my own, the following note, expressing his lively
thanks for an act of common friendship :—

"London, Sept. 11, 1855.

" My dear Caswall,

" Your letter is a great lift by the way.   The interest which you have manifested in me and my poor
labours, while it greatly encourages me, endears you
more than ever to my poor heart, and fills it with gratitude imperishable. I see, by the tenor of the bishop's
note, what you have written, and I do hope you will
consent to its being forwarded to Barbados and published.   It will disarm the opponents of our mission,
warm and rejoice the hearts of its friends, awake the
sleepers, and stir up a lively interest in its favour, and
in the cause of missions generally.

" I am now in great trouble, having much baggage to take along with me, and freight-charges which almost cover its real value. In this country it would be hardly worth the cost, in Africa it will be indispensable. I have to submit.

"I have just returned from the Bishop (of Sierra Leone's) residence, — a long, long walk, and back again,—all to save our association a few pence. The bishop was with the Archbishop of Canterbury, and I had to leave my papers and a message at his house.

"Yours sincerely," &c.

On the 20th Mr. Leacock returned to us from London. Great was our joy when his noble and manly form entered our house, when we heard his cheerful laugh, and received the cordial shake of his hand.

"It is pleasing to see in experience," remarks a recent writer,* "that oftentimes the men of most depth and seriousness of character, — the men who in their closets take the most earnest view of life, and have cultivated heavenly wisdom most largely, have also been men of lively fancy, sprightly and agreeable repartee, seem to have had within them a spring of joy and merriment bubbling up when the obstruction of serious affairs was removed, and covering with fertility even the leisure hours of their lives. The world's wisest men have mingled mirth with earnestness,— they have not gone about with starched visage, prim manner, or puritanical grimace." This character applies in every particular to the friend whom it was now our happiness to welcome.

* Goulburn : "The Idle Word," p. 86.

Speaking, about this time, of books, Mr. Leacock expressed his admiration of Thomas à Kempis, and Bunyan's Pilgrim's Progress. He mentioned having parted with the copy of à Kempis, which I had given him in Kentucky, at the earnest solicitation of one of his parishioners in Perth Amboy, who had formed an attachment to the book. I now presented him with another copy, which he received with great delight, and took with him to Africa.

He was a man of few books. His well-worn Bible was the companion of all his wanderings, and an unfailing source of consolation. During this visit it was delightful to observe the intense enjoyment which he derived from his religion. He seemed to have risen above the murky region of anxieties, apprehensions, doubts, and fears, and to be cheerfully reposing in the calm sunshine of divine love. He had severed most of the ties which bound him to the world, and was already looking forward with happy anticipations to his entrance into rest.

He would often, at this time, collect around him a party of young persons, and rivet their attention by his conversation and by his dramatic action. Sometimes he would talk of hurricanes until his youthful hearers seemed to hear the fury of the wind, and to feel themselves involved in its terrific whirls. He would vividly describe the shaking of an earthquake, representing the concussion of the trees and houses, and the frantic rushing forth of the inhabitants. He would speak of the terrors of the cholera, and show how the people quailed at the approach of the invisible enemy; how they attempted to flee, and were arrested in their flight, and miserably perished. In one moment he would weep bitterly when he spoke of his wife's decease, and in another moment he would fix his mind on some glorious prophecy, and speak with rapture of the future triumphs of the Gospel. Then he would talk solemnly of wonderful providences which had fallen within the range of his experience; of the death-beds of pirates, slave-hunters, atheists, and murderers; and how even such wretches as these had confessed to him their crimes, and thrown themselves on the mercy of God in Christ. Again, changing the subject, he would speak of the beauties of the West Indies; of the lovely islands reposing on the bosom of the sea, or of the noble forests and rivers of America. From these subjects he would suddenly digress to the many mansions prepared for Christians in the house of their Father, the blessedness of Paradise, the trees of life, and the river that makes glad the city of God.

Like many other earnest Christians, he had paid a large share of attention to the subject of prophecy, and was generally inclined to adopt a literal interpretation. As might be expected from his habits and education, he took but little interest in many of our existing controversies. Without manifesting bigotry or prejudice on the subject, he cared little for questions pertaining to ecclesiastical vestments, liturgical minutiæ, crosses, candlesticks, or church architecture. As for the Roman Catholic religion, while he greatly admired the writings of saints like Thomas à Kempis,

OPINION OF THE VOLUNTARY SYSTEM.

he considered the system of Popery to be clearly condemned by the word of God.

He viewed with slight apprehensions the assaults of the enemies of the Church of England, believing her, in her essential parts, to be founded on a rock. He even thought it probable that the downfall of the present establishment in this island would, if permitted, be made to result in the lasting good of the English Episcopal Church. He viewed State connexion and royal supremacy only as the accidents of a certain portion of our reformed communion. He thought well of the "voluntary system" (so called) as practised by the American Church, believing that under it, as a general rule, clergymen who do their duty faithfully, do not want any thing *really* necessary. He considered self-denial and faith the best endowments of the ministry, and a readiness to endure hardship as better than all tithes or rent-charges. He firmly maintained that if men would honestly seek in the first place the kingdom of God and his righteousness, other things would be added unto them. He agreed, in short, with the speaker who said in the American General Convention, "In regard to a clergyman and his support, it is like a man and his shadow in the sun. If he runs towards his shadow, it flies before him; if he goes *towards the sun*, the shadow will follow close upon his heels."

It must be recollected that Mr. Leacock had hitherto been a stranger to England, and that many points in our established Church system were entirely new to him. Had he remained here longer, it is probable that, in a few respects, he would have found reason to change his mind. He would have seen, for example, that the endowments of the Church of England are but the effects of a voluntary system operating through a long course of ages, and protected by a Christian legislature.

He thought our clergy were too much subject to routine, and to conventional habits. It grieved him to read in the "Ecclesiastical Gazette" of so many ministers of Christ seeking comfortable benefices at home instead of going forth manfully into the wide Pagan and Mohammedan world with the message of salvation. He viewed self-renunciation as an essential feature of a truly Christian ministry. In giving up his own home in Barbados, and in going to labour in Africa, he felt that he was doing nothing more than what ought to be reasonably expected of a priest of the true Church.

He expressed himself unspeakably thankful to God for the goodness and mercy which had followed him all the days of his life. In the present instance he viewed it as a great mercy that Providence had sent into England one of his old Kentucky friends to receive him, and to forward the objects of his mission. And I recollect with pleasure that he quoted as a favourite that well-known hymn which forms a part of the American collection :—

> "When all thy mercies, O my God,
>   My rising soul surveys,
>   Transported with the view I'm lost
>   In wonder, love, and praise.

NOTE ON THE EFFECTS OF EMANCIPATION.

" When in the slipp'ry paths of youth
With heedless steps I ran,
Thine arm, unseen, convey'd me safe,
And led me up to man.

" Through hidden dangers, toils, and deaths,
It gently clear'd the way,
And through the pleasing snares of vice,
More to be fear'd than they. •

" Ten thousand thousand precious gifts
My daily thanks employ ;
Nor is the least a cheerful heart
That tastes those gifts with joy.

" Through all enternity, to Thee
A joyful song I'll raise ;
But, oh ! eternity's too short
To utter all thy praise."

NOTE TO CHAPTER V.

Mr. Leacock having expressed himself, while in England, somewhat doubtfully as to the results of slave-emancipation in the West Indies, I wrote to the Bishop of Barbados on the subject, and obtained the following answer, dated at St. Vincent, Dec. 11, 1856.

" I do not consider Mr. Leacock to have been correct in thinking that emancipation has not advanced the negroes in industry and morals. The effect was to give freer play to both the good and the evil tendencies of the negro. Some became worse, others better. On the whole, the social improvement has been great, especially in Barbados. The island never produced so much as it does now : nor were the people, throughout all classes, ever so comfortable, so orderly and civilized, nor, I think, so industrious. There is more crime; all offences against the law coming now under public cognizance, not, as heretofore, under that of the proprietor or his representative; and though there is much immorality, still it must be remembered that there was scarcely any thing else formerly among the slaves, to say nothing of their masters. Other colonies have had greater difficulties to contend with than Barbados ; but, in all, the general result in the character of the people has been for good."

CHAPTER VI.

Providential Preparation in Africa for the West Indian Mission. The Chief Wilkinson introduced. Remarkable Dream in Africa. Mr. Leacock attends various Meetings in the Diocese of Salisbury. He meets with a Portrait of Mrs. Trimmer. Verses by Mr. Marriott. Mr. Leacock's opinion of the S.P.G. He visits Malvern and the Bishop of Barbados. His Admiration of England. His Feelings in Wells Cathedral. He embarks at Plymouth for Africa.

LEAVING Mr. Leacock for a short time in Wiltshire, it may be well in this place to notice the events which had prepared the way for him in Africa.

About a hundred and forty miles to the northward of Sierra Leone, in the tenth degree of latitude, and the fourteenth of longitude, west of Greenwich, the Fattalah river enters the Atlantic ocean. This beautiful river was long the favourite resort of slave-traders, whose vessels lay concealed among its numerous creeks while the cargoes of wretched Africans were being secretly embarked. The soil of the neighbouring country is exceedingly fertile, and maintains a large population, though the climate is generally fatal to Europeans. The people are, for the most part, idolatrous heathens, but Mohammedan teachers

THE CHIEF WILKINSON.

have much influence over them. As might be expected, the grossest superstitions are prevalent, as well as the most deplorable laxity of morals. The villages contain about four or five hundred inhabitants each, the dwelling-houses being constructed in a style of architecture which gives them the appearance of bee-hives. There is usually a chief over every village, who acts very independently of external control.

At about four miles from the bar at its mouth, the Fattalah river divides into two streams The northeastern of these is denominated the Big Pongas, or simply the Fattalah, and divides again into the Fattalah proper and the Bangalong. The south-eastern branch of the main stream is called the Rio Pongas, and sometimes the Little Pongas. At the distance of nine miles from the bar, on the northern bank of the Little Pongas, is the village of Tintima. About twelve miles higher up the same stream, and on the northern bank of a small tributary creek called the Fallaniah, is Fallangia, a village of five hundred and thirty inhabitants, the present chief of which, although a perfect African, bears the English name of Richard Wilkinson.

Wilkinson was born about the year 1795, nearly at the same time with Mr. Leacock. Early in life he was brought to England, where he acquired the rudiments of a Christian education, and learned to speak and write the English language. Returning to his native land, he fell back into a state of practical heathenism, and adopted again the customs of his

5

REMARKABLE DREAM.

countrymen. It pleased God, however, in the year
1835, to afflict him with a dangerous illness. His re-
collections of England and of the Christian religion
now revived, and his awakened conscience accused
him of many offences in the sight of his Maker. He
determined, in the event of his recovery, to pray
daily to God that a missionary might be sent to teach
him and his people the way of salvation. Being
raised up from his sick bed he put this resolution in
practice, and, in the autumn of 1855, his prayers had
continued to ascend during twenty years without any
prospect of the long-desired missionary's approach.

About the beginning of October, however, while
Mr. Leacock was in England, a remarkable event occurred which the reader will regard as either a strange
coincidence or as a special interposition of Him who
wills that all men should come to a knowledge of the
truth. A son of the chief Wilkinson and of a woman
called "Old Martha" had a dream, which he mentioned to his parents in the presence of several other
persons. He said, "Father, a missionary is coming.
I saw him in a dream walking from the landing-place
to this house." Like the ancient races of mankind,
the people of the Pongas country place great confidence in dreams, and this dream was received as an
indication from heaven that the prayers of the old
chief were about to be answered.

Meanwhile the missionary, who was destined to
fulfil the premonitory dream in every particular, was
making known the object of his mission in several
places within the diocese of Salisbury. On the 24th

of September we were invited by the Rev. F. Bennett to attend a missionary meeting at Maddington, where Mr. Leacock spoke with great power and effect. On the following day we proceeded to Devizes, where he was engaged to address a meeting of the neighbouring gentry convened at the Assembly-room. Several unpleasant circumstances combined to damp his spirits, and his faculty of utterance seemed almost to have forsaken him. He merely spoke a few words and sat down, much distressed, under the apprehension that his failure would injuriously affect his mission. For some days his spirits continued greatly depressed; but on the 28th, after much solicitation, he consented to take a part in the annual meeting at Figheldean in behalf of the Society for Propagating the Gospel. The parishioners and the neighbouring clergy evincing a warm interest in Africa, Mr. Leacock felt the genial effect of sympathy, and delivered an address which moved every heart by its solemnity and pathetic eloquence. This was followed by a most impressive sermon delivered in Figheldean Church on the 30th, the day appointed for the thanksgiving on account of the capture of Sebastopol. On this occasion one of the hearers remarked, "Surely the Apostle Paul has revisited the world in the person of Mr. Leacock."

On the 3rd of October we called at the residence of a lady, Miss Crane, who had erected a monument to the memory of Mrs. Trimmer, by means of a penny subscription. Here Mr. Leacock was shown a picture of the good old authoress, which he kissed with enthusiasm in memory of the little book which had first

VERSES BY MR. MARRIOTT.

impressed his mind with ideas of religious duty. The following verses by Mr. Marriott about this time met his eye, and he requested one of my children to copy them, in order that he might take them to Africa.

"Casting all your care upon Him, for He careth for you."—1 Pet. v. 7.

"For me? was it rightly I heard?
    Oh! hope too presumptuous, I fear;
Let the sweet, the encouraging word
    Still dwell on my gratified ear.

"On my *ear*, did I say? little gain,
    Little comfort such gift would impart.
Oh! let its deep impress remain
    Indelibly stamp'd on my *heart*.

"Does God then his creatures invite
    Upon *Him* to cast every care?
His word does Omnipotence plight
    Thus freely their burden to bear?

"Oh! let me not baffle such love
    By a thoughtless and cold unbelief;
But my love and my gratitude prove
    By resigning my every grief.

"Does *He* then his fostering hand
    In mercy from heaven extend;
And shall *I* such compassion withstand,
    And refuse such a bountiful Friend?

"Let me rather with rapture embrace
    An offer so gracious aud kind,
And unlimited confidence place
    In such power and such goodness combined.

"To the heart truly humbled by woe,
    The anointing of joy shall be given;
To the tears that from penitence flow,
    The peace that's a foretaste of heaven."

On the last occasion of his attending family worship with us, the following hymn, from the selection of the late Bishop of Salisbury, was sung at his request, his own voice joining with peculiar fervour :—

> " Blest be thy love, good Lord,
>   That taught us this sweet way;
> Only to love Thee for Thyself,
>   And for that love obey.
>
> " O Thou, our soul's chief hope,
>   We to thy mercy fly ;
> Where'er we are Thou canst protect,
>   Whate'er we need, supply.
>
> " Whether we sleep or wake,
>   To Thee we both resign ;
> By night we see, as well as day,
>   If thy light on us shine.
>
> " Whether we live or die,
>   Both we submit to Thee ;
> In death we live, as well as life,
>   If thine in death we be."

On the fifth of October Mr. Leacock left us and went to the Rev. Mr. Bennett's at Maddington. On the 8th I met him at Amesbury, at the hospitable abode of the Rev. Prebendary Fowle. On that evening a very interesting missionary meeting took place in which he bore a most effective part. After the conclusion of the meeting he returned to Maddington, and I saw his face no more.

Mr. Bennett thus expresses his opinion of Mr. Leacock's character :—

" That he was chosen of God, and almost inspired for the work, I fully felt while I had the privilege of receiving him as my guest. I felt persuaded that he was especially fitted for the work of founding a mission, because he was animated by a martyr's spirit, and believed himself moved by the Holy Ghost to go to Africa.

"Until he came to England he had misunderstood the Church movement of the present day, and his thankfulness was great for being undeceived on this and various other points by what he had seen for himself in this country. It was quite pleasing to hear the cordial gratitude which he expressed to the Society for Propagating the Gospel and its officers for the heartiness with which they received him, and the testimony he gave to the entire freedom from any thing approaching to party spirit in their proceedings. Having received his education at the hands of that Society in Codrington College, it was, he said, a great pleasure to find her members animated, one and all, so far as he had an opportunity of judging from personal observation, by the best and purest spirit of Christian charity, and anxious to know no party but the Church of England."

The following letter from Mr. Leacock, dated at Bristol, October 17th, is too striking to be omitted :--

"My dear Caswall,

"You are perhaps wondering what has become of your old friend; and well you may, for I have been moving ever since we parted on Monday evening at Amesbury. That may be the last time we shall meet this side of eternity; and if it should so prove, I am

THE BISHOP OF BARBADOS. 103

thankful that we parted in the bonds of true Christian
love, such as shall be matured in heaven. The next
day found me at Norton Bavant, with my honoured
and esteemed old archdeacon. I could not long enjoy
this happy rest; but, accompanied by the dear old
man and his daughter the next day to Warminster, I
took the railway for Bristol, where I arrived in the
afternoon too late for a good opportunity to Worcester. I reached that place next day at twelve o'clock,
and Malvern Wells at three P.M., where I passed two
days with my good bishop.* I trust he will return to
his diocese in May greatly strengthened by his visit
to England.

"I received letters on Friday which rendered it
necessary that I should tarry in Malvern no longer;
and so, instead of two weeks at Malvern Wells, I
passed only two days, engaged partly in business with
the bishop, and, when the rain would admit, rambling
with him on the neighbouring mountains, and enjoy-
ing the most beautiful views of nature—not a formal-
looking artificial thing on canvas, but the most beautiful views of nature that eye ever beheld. Old England is indeed a personification of all that is now
lovely in nature or art to be found on earth. Other
places seem to me but copies. I have no doubt, however, that the giant infant in the West will one day
or other take off her shine, and perhaps undutifully
kick her into the shade.

"But, as usual, here I am *rambling*. I must go

* The Bishop of Barbados.

104   FEELINGS IN WELLS CATHEDRAL.

back to Malvern.   On Saturday morning, *right early*, I was ready to start, when, having taken alone an early breakfast, the bell rang for prayers, and down came the bishop and all his family.   We sang a hymn, read a very suitable psalm, and knelt down.   The bishop's prayer was most devout and affecting.   We all felt it.   The postilion's horn sounded just before we had said the last ' Amen ; ' and, my hands grasped by each individual, I bid farewell—a hurried farewell —to Malvern, with no expectation of ever beholding it again.

"We reached Worcester in less than two hours,— and, settled on the railway, we puffed, and steamed, and screamed, and raged, and roared, as hard as ever John Bull could go, and reached dirty Bristol in three hours ; and, having got some refreshment, we started again for Somersetshire, and reached Wells at seven o'clock in the evening.

"The next day I attended service at the Cathedral ; and at six o'clock dined, according to invitation, with Mr. Canon Pinder.   He seemed rejoiced to see me, and said that he knew me the moment he put his eye on me in the Cathedral.   A more cordial welcome I could not have received from *you*.   He talked till a late hour, deeply interested about every thing Barbadian or West Indian.   I would not have missed the interview with him on any account.

"But one of the most important circumstances connected with this visit was the services of the Cathedral.   They have left an impression on my heart which, I believe, can never be entirely obliterated.

FEELINGS IN WELLS CATHEDRAL. 105

To *my mind* there was a something peculiar in them, which was probably unfelt and unnoticed by any of the congregation present. As in the case of Saul going to Damascus on his bloody purpose, none of his companions saw the vision, or heard the heavenly voice that spoke to him—none so impressed as he, or had such cause to remember the events of that day as he —so it is *possible* it may be with me. None could see as I saw, nor hear as I heard, in the Cathedral on that day. The services, I say, were remarkable; just suited to one going on my mission, and seeming as if prepared for the occasion of my visit, and intended as a farewell. You will say, 'It is all visionary and nonsense,' and probably many would say so too; but if God was pleased to affect my mind in that peculiar manner, I can't help it; and if He was pleased to comfort and encourage me in my undertaking by such means, *I*, at least, cannot regard it as nonsense or visionary. The text in the morning was the 6th of 1 Cor. 20, in which the preacher, one of the Canons, set before us a great duty, viz. *to glorify God*—how it was to be performed, viz. *in your body and in your spirit*—and lastly, the reasons which rendered the performance of the duty absolutely necessary, 'Ye are not your own, ye are bought with a price; your body and spirit are God's.' He treated the subject in a plain and forcible manner, and concluded with exhorting all to make a surrender of themselves to God, and devote themselves to his service. And he moreover exhorted them not only to give up their bodies and souls to God's service, but also to devote their in-

5*

fluence and wealth to Him by sending the Gospel to nations that have it not, and encouraging by their sympathy, and helping by their wealth and prayers, those men who had already gone, or were preparing to go forth, to the dark and cruel places of the earth. I was amazed; but how much more so when, in the afternoon service, from another Canon, I heard a very plain, affecting, and most profitable sermon from Dan. vi. 10. The chapter was the first lesson. The preacher not only warned all men of the dangers of the Christian warfare in a civilized country; but, in a special manner, of the dangers which attend the propagation of the Gospel in heathen lands, where persecution rages openly; and, pointing to the example of the noble and upright Daniel, exhorted all Christians to pray continually, for our strength lay only in God, and He could easily shut the lions' mouths. He spoke also of missions, and of the necessity of all Christians, and especially missionaries, to set their face as a flint, and fear nothing; to be strong in the Lord and in the power of his might; to desire life only to serve God and benefit man, and not to fear death; for while thus engaged, death would be a friend to remove us from the scenes and troubles of this evil world. It was sweet encouragement to me—it was good for me to be there—better a thousand times than if it had been known that I was to be there, or if the services had been appointed as a farewell. I felt that God, not man, had ordered the services, and brought me to hear them. I may be wrong, but I only tell you what

I felt. If wrong, I pray that my folly and presumption may be forgiven.

"But what shall I say of the Psalms for the morning (14th day of the month), every verse teeming with something that worked powerfully and variously in me? The 71st setting forth David's confidence and prayer for perseverance, and the 72nd showing the greatness, goodness, and glory of Christ's kingdom; all affording great encouragement in the work of missions, as did the sermon in the morning; and the Psalms of the evening service, showing the dangers of the Christian warfare, and the necessity of prayer, as did the sermon at the same service. The Psalms exactly suited to the sermons, or rather the sermons to the Psalms, struck me with power.

"But the singing. Oh! the singing was heavenly. The choir was below, not in the gallery, eight men and eight boys. All the parts were well sustained. But there was a voice which penetrated my ear, and sank into my heart. I could distinguish it easily in the chorus; but when *it* was heard in a solo the book and my hands dropped on the pew. I thought I should have fallen down. But I nerved myself as well as I could. I looked at the sweet cherubic little chorister, and his meek, gentle eyes were *fixed upon me*, while his soft music flowed sweetly from him without an apparent effort, and was heard penetrating the wide extent of the great building. The child kept his eyes upon me, and drew tears abundantly from mine. It was my own Mary's voice, her own sweet, impressive mode of singing, as she was wont to sing in her early days when I first knew her. I sat down, hid my tearful eyes in my handkerchief during the rest of the service, and cannot refrain from tears even now, and whenever that voice rings in my ears.

"God bless you, my dear friend, and your wife and your children. May your heart never bleed as does mine.

"Affectionately yours."

In the mean time, Mrs. Caswall and my family, with the help of our neighbours and parishioners, were preparing a box of articles likely to be useful to Mr. Leacock in Africa. On the 18th of October he addressed Mrs. Caswall as follows, from Bristol:—

"My dear Mrs. Caswall,

"By this time you are so heartily tired of my scribbling that I question whether you will tolerate this letter. You must have received one this morning from me to Caswall, by which you had some account of my journeyings. I cannot say that they have been attended, like Paul's, with 'weariness and painfulness,' for I have had nothing to do but sit down quietly, and be whisked along as fast as steam could do it; nor can I say, 'with hungering and thirsting,' for I have had plenty of good care.

"I do hope that Providence may yet give me a few months in England after my business is done in Africa. It would afford me much gratification to walk about your village, and talk to the people about the good things which are prepared for them that love God. But such an event is far, far ahead—far below our present horizon, and may never, never rise to our view. But whatever God does will be right, and that is enough for me. He knows, at a glance, all that is before us, and I am quite satisfied to wait the issue of events.

" It is quite a gratification to me to hear that those good people at Netheravon, Mr. and Mrs. Blandy, have in remembrance me and my mission to · Africa. I hope my mission will always be entertained by them and all God's people with favourable regard, and that, *through the Divine blessing on my labours*, I may be enabled to send from Africa such tidings to them as will rejoice their hearts, and reward them for the sacrifice they have already offered, and for the further sacrifices which God may incline them to offer. Thanking you, my dear Mrs. Caswall, for your hospitality and kindness to me, and praying God, as I do daily, to bless you and your dear husband, and all your children, and all who show me kindness,

"I remain, &c."

From Bristol Mr. Leacock proceeded to Plymouth; where he met his companion Duport, and on the 24th of October embarked with him on board the "Ethiope" steamer for Sierra Leone. They were fellow-passengers with Dr. Weeks, the new bishop of Sierra Leone, under whose direction and superintendence their work was to be commenced and prosecuted. The Rev. Mr. Pocock, the assistant colonial chaplain of Sierra Leone, was also on board, together with his lady.

EMBARKATION AT PLYMOUTH.

There were likewise other clergymen connected with the Church Missionary Society, besides some candidates for Holy Orders. Just before sailing, Mr. Leacock wrote to me the following note :—

"I have only time to say, I thank you and your dear wife for your letters, for the box, for the precious things which it contains, and for all your good wishes, which I know are sincere. Farewell, my dear brother; may the Lord bless you, your dear wife and your children, and bring us all to meet together before his throne of glory, there to praise and adore Him for ever, through Jesus Christ our Saviour."

CHAPTER VII.

Voyage of the "Ethiope." Dangerous Storm. Arrival at Madeira. Warm Reception by a Governor on the African Coast. Arrival at Sierra Leone. Description of Freetown. Various Opinions as to the Site of the Mission. Similarity of Sierra Leone to the West Indies. Joy at the Discovery of Devil-grass. Dr. Bradshaw's advice as to a House. The Niger Considered. Plaintain Island and John Newton. Further Delay. Interview with the Spanish Consul. Meeting of the Church Missionary Society.

UPON embarking in the "Ethiope" at Plymouth, Mr. Leacock was far from satisfied with the appearance of the vessel. He remarked to a clergyman who had come on board with him, "This ship is too narrow in the beam for her length, and she is also too deep in the water; if we encounter a heavy sea she will be in great danger." The gentleman smiled at this remark, not being aware of Mr. Leacock's long experience in matters of this description. The sequel showed that the veteran missionary was in the right.

At night, on Wednesday 24th, the anchor was weighed, and the vessel, a screw-propeller, advanced for some time rapidly through the smooth water. On Thursday the wind became contrary, and the ship

112   DANGEROUS STORM.

rolling awfully, almost every person on board suffered
from sea-sickness. On Friday, the wind being still
adverse and blowing pretty hard, they got abreast of
the Bay of Biscay. About four o'clock in the afternoon, while Mr. Leacock was in his berth, a sea
struck the ship and broke heavily over her. The
water was up to the top of the bulwarks, about five
feet deep on the lee-side, and washed away whatever
was not well secured. A young sailor was carried
overboard and two of the passengers narrowly escaped.
The vessel was stopped in the hope of saving the unhappy seaman, but the waves soon covered and en-
gulphed him. At this moment another sea struck
the vessel on the quarter, and floated away every
thing that could float in the saloon and in all the
berths. Boots, shoes, slippers, clothes, bags, portman-
teaus, &c., were floating all night, and all perfectly
saturated.

The ship was full of passengers. In Mr. Leacock's
state-room there were three. One of these was a
German in Holy Orders, a gentle, kind, young man,
ready to assist Mr. Leacock to the uttermost of his
power. He was going to the African coast in the
service of the Church Missionary Society. While
Mr. Leacock was confined to his berth by illness, this
good brother sat by his side, morning and evening,
sometimes reading to him and sometimes offering up
prayers.

Meanwhile the vessel rolled along, but could not
make much way. She was unable to carry her usual
quantity of steam, which would soon have buried her

ARRIVAL AT MADEIRA.

beneath the waves. The captain was content to lay her to occasionally; and when proceeding during the gale he did not allow the vessel to make more than a mile or a mile and a half an hour.

On All Saints' Day, the 1st of November, they arrived at Funchal in Madeira, from whence Mr. Leacock immediately wrote me a letter containing the above particulars. "You can now thank God," he added, "for having heard your prayers and delivered me from the horrid yawning gulf of Biscay. We have passed through many dangers, but I was kept in perfect peace, knowing Who was at the helm. Now, thank God, we are all safe. The passengers are gone on shore, and I am alone. Whether I shall go or not, I have not yet decided. It is most likely that I shall remain. The same clothes I wore when I came on board I have on still. All were wet, and when dried they looked worse than if they had been worn. In the top of my portmanteau I hoped to find a dry shirt, but when I opened it this morning every thing was wet through, and stained by the leather, which looks very filthy. This then is my present position. I have nothing to state about the prospects of my mission. The bishop says it is likely we shall be able to decide on some place when we are in Sierra Leone. Till then, farewell."

Leaving Madeira, the "Ethiope" proceeded by Goree to the African coast, and touched in the first place at a settlement considerably northward of Sierra Leone. The English governor of this settlement had married a lady formerly connected with one of Mr.

Leacock's congregations in the West Indies. She had recently died; but her mention of Mr. Leacock as her good and faithful pastor in former days had made a deep impression on the mind of her husband. While the " Ethiope " was coaling and landing a portion of her cargo, Mr. Leacock was hospitably entertained at the governor's residence, where he was treated with the utmost respect and consideration. After passing a night on shore and leading the family devotions of the worthy governor and his household, he returned on board the vessel and proceeded on his voyage down the coast.

On the 10th of November Mr. Leacock came in sight of Sierra Leone. The peninsula to which this name is attached appeared like a number of hills irregularly heaped together. On a nearer approach his eye was delighted with the grandeur and beauty of the scenery formed by these hills, and the valleys and prairies discovered in the intervals. Lofty forests clothed the mountains and lent an air of richness and luxuriance to the landscape.[*]

Freetown, the capital of the colony, stands about five miles from the northern extremity of the peninsula, on the south side of a noble estuary called the River Sierra Leone. Here the " Ethiope " entered a fine bay, affording excellent anchorage not only for steamers, but for vessels of every class. Mr. Leacock perceived that the town was handsomely situated, occupying a piece of ground gradually ascending for three

---

[*] See the Rev. S. A. Walker's "Church of England Missions in Sierra Leone."

ARRIVAL AT SIERRA LEONE.

quarters of a mile from the sea till it reached the foot of the mountains. To the left the shore is broken into a series of little bays with moderate hills, gently rising above and waving with palm-trees.. In front the wide Sierra Leone River, bordered by low woods, glitters in the constant sunshine. Half-way up the side of a hill may be seen the fort, the barracks, the hospital, the government house, and a martello tower, the whole forming a prospect of surpassing beauty.

The town is regularly laid out with fine streets eighty feet wide, intersecting each other at right angles. Each house has a piazza, with pillars at regular intervals, supporting verandahs which afford a shady walk even when the noon-day sun is shining. The dwellings are surrounded with gardens, and shaded with trees which receive the cool breezes blowing from the wide Atlantic.

At the foot of the rocky heights which suddenly break upon the regularity of the streets, are long suburbs occupied by emancipated slaves, and constituting the most extensive and populous part of Freetown. These suburbs present an appearance of great meanness and poverty, the huts being formed of a few stakes fixed in the ground, wattled together, and plastered with brown mud. Attached to these huts are small patches of ground in which the papaw, plaintain, and banana are cultivated.

The principal church has been denominated the Cathedral since the consecration of a bishop. It is a spacious building, and was constructed entirely by emancipated negroes and boys under Christian instruction, superintended by a single European.

The bishop had faithfully laboured as a missionary in this colony during the early part of his life, and therefore found himself at home among many old associations. Mr. Leacock made his way to the post-office, in order to despatch to England and the West Indies the news of his safe arrival. The post-mistress, on seeing him, at once addressed him by name, and manifested strong emotions of delight. She informed him that while a little child, she had lived in a family at Nevis, which Mr. Leacock had been in the habit of visiting. He had kindly noticed this child a quarter of a century before, and now the same person rejoiced to welcome him to the shores of Africa, and desired to show him every attention in her power. His satisfaction at the unexpected meeting was reciprocal, and even in this apparently trivial coincidence he saw the sign of a good providence going before him and preparing his way.

The reader is aware that Archdeacon Trew of the Bahamas, had given Mr. Leacock a letter to Lieutenant-Colonel Hill, the governor of the colony. Sir William Colebrooke had shown him a similar attention, and in addition to this Her Majesty's Government had faithfully fulfilled the promise given in 1851. One of the latest official acts of the late Secretary of State, Sir William Molesworth, was to recommend Mr. Leacock and his work to the countenance and protection of the several English governors on the coast of Western Africa.

VARIOUS OPINIONS. 117

Col. Hill received the good missionary with the utmost courtesy and respect, and invited him to dine at Government House soon after his arrival. This kindness penetrated his heart, and from that time he recognized in the governor a steady friend and benefactor. Conversing with his Excellency in regard to the best point for the establishment of the West Indian Mission, Mr. Leacock, in the first instance, was recommended to visit Cape Coast Castle, and to examine the district called El-Mina, in which there is a Dutch settlement, about seven miles north of the fortification just mentioned. In a subsequent conversation, the governor stated that further consideration had induced him to think less favourably of El-Mina, and proceeded to advise Mr. Leacock to remain within British territory. "There is plenty of room," he said, " in our government for another mission, and we want labourers. Why then leave us for a foreign government? Under British influence you may be sure of protection; and while you are labouring for the salvation of a benighted people you may render us an essential service. Plantain Island and all the Sherbro' country down to the Gallinas lie open before you, nearly seventy miles in breadth, and extending far up into the interior. There is no Church mission here. Certain portions of the country are almost depopulated by the slave-hunters, and slave-trade. The chiefs are ever at war with each other, and no moral or religious influence has been brought to bear upon them. That, in my mind, seems to be the place for the West Indian Mission, and it will in time fill up the gap between the British and the American settlements."

This was the substance of his Excellency's remarks, which he offered in the kindest manner, as the result of his mature deliberation. Mr. Leacock immediately communicated them to the Bishop of Sierra Leone, who expressed his entire approbation of the governor's views.

While awaiting in Freetown an opportunity of visiting the Sherbro' country, Mr. Leacock was far from idle. On the 25th of November he preached to a large congregation of natives who understood a little English. They joined readily in the service, but, in certain parts of it, in such a manner as induced him to think it would be lost labour to *read* a sermon, and accordingly he preached *extempore*. He easily perceived by the earnest attention of all, and the sighs and groans of many, the deep interest which they took in what was said, and he had the satisfaction afterwards of learning that he was distinctly understood.

The bishop attended the cathedral in the morning, and during the Litany fell down in a state of insensibility, and was carried home immediately. Although Mr. Pocock, his chaplain, was ready to officiate, the bishop had preferred to take the entire duty himself, and suffered accordingly.

Mr. Leacock was at this time disposed to think favourably of Sierra Leone, and his own health and Duport's continued excellent. "I am persuaded," he wrote to the Bishop of Barbados, "that one is not

SIERRA LEONE LIKE THE WEST INDIES. 119

more exposed to disease in Sierra Leone than in the
West Indies. The scenery, the trees, the shrubbery,
the fruit, the flowers, the climate, the people; every
thing and person reminds me of home. Even devil-
grass (called here Bahama-grass), the pest and plague
of our Barbados planters, is here. It was among the
first things that attracted my notice, and for the first
time in my life I was delighted to behold it. While
I am writing the sun is shining in his strength; but
in the house it is cool and pleasant. I have seen
nothing yet of Africa which I contemplated at home.
But Sierra Leone is said to be the *garden*—I will tell
you about the *wilderness* when I get into it.

"We have here a Dr. Bradshaw, a worthy son of
the 'Green Isle.' He tells me that I must have the
floor of my house raised from the ground at least six
feet to keep me from the damp, and the roof covered
with shingles, and then the only caution necessary for
the preservation of my health is, what every prudent
man observes in all tropical countries—*temperance*
and *exercise.* I hope the committee will be able to
assist me in erecting such a building. It will have
only four rooms in it, a gallery, an entrance-room, a
parlour, and two bed-rooms. A cottage for the schoolmaster must be separate, two comfortable rooms and
a piazza. I beg your lordship to inform the committee
that their missionaries cannot exist in a low, hot,
smoky cottage, such as the natives inhabit, having a
damp earthen floor, wattled and mud-plastered walls
and partitions, and straw-covered roofs, for the preservation of which fire must be made in the centre of

120 THE NIGER CONSIDERED.

the building to destroy or expel scorpions, and centipedes, and small insects, which generate in the straw and destroy it, making in a few weeks a thousand channels for the rain. Self-preservation will prompt me, in building a house, to consult our missionaries' health, while I have a due regard to the most rigid economy. I trust the management of the means committed by the society to my care has not shaken their confidence in my economy. As soon as I can ascertain where I am to be fixed, and what sum is necessary for the erection of our cottage, I shall write to my old friend Dr. Caswall and other friends in England for help; and shall leave your lordship to lay the matter before the Propagation Society and the committee of our association. I shall do what I can to get assistance from the natives on the spot; and you may rely on it, I shall spend no more in building than is absolutely necessary for the protection of our health. And this I shall do promptly, for, if I resolve to await the arrival of your sanction, I may not live to receive it."

On the 28th of the same month (November), after a long conversation with a clergyman respecting the Sherbro' country, Mr. Leacock was asked whether he was willing to go up the Niger, as far as the junction of the Chadda, and open his mission there. He replied, that he was at the disposal of the Bishop of Sierra Leone, and that he would most willingly go if the bishop would send him. The bishop, however, strongly dissuaded him from such an undertaking, and said, "Do not entertain such a thought for a moment. All that coast is infested with pirates and murderers, and, without a guard, a man's life is in danger. The river is not open. There is no communication but through Fernandó Po, and the expense of ascending so high up as the Chadda in canoes would be enormous."

In the mean time the governor's favourable opinion respecting Sherbro' and Plantain Islands had been shaken by a Mr. McCormack, who had recently travelled through that district, and accordingly he invited Mr. Leacock to meet this gentleman at dinner. In the course of conversation Mr. McCormack said that nothing could be done in Plantain Island. It was a desolation. The fire and sword of the neighbouring chiefs, spurred on by the Portuguese slave-hunters, had driven away the inhabitants who had escaped the chains of slavery, and spread ruin throughout the country.

Plantain Island was a scene in the celebrated John Newton's early life, and is still one of the greatest slave markets on the coast. More than a hundred years have passed since Newton was a wretched wanderer in this island. Old people were, however, living there in 1837 who remembered him, and some aged lime-trees were still growing which had been planted by the hand of this celebrated convert.

Newton records a curious circumstance respecting his life on Plantain Island. "One thing, though strange, is most true. Though destitute of food and clothing, depressed to a degree beyond common wretchedness, I could sometimes collect my mind to mathematical studies. I had bought Barrow's Euclid at Portsmouth; it was the only volume I brought on shore; it was always with me, and I used to take it to remote corners of the island by the sea-side, and draw my diagrams with a long stick upon the sand."

Mr. Leacock, though discouraged by his kind friend the governor, still entertained the idea of visiting this beautiful island, in order to ascertain whether any inhabitants remained. He was now becoming anxious about his prospects, and wrote to the Bishop of Barbados as follows: "The whole *accessible* ground on the coast is already occupied by missionaries. Nothing, therefore, seems to remain for me but a struggle with the proud conceited Mohammedan, who is also cunning, crafty, malicious, a bitter enemy to Christianity, and indefatigable in his efforts to propagate the dogmas of his creed among the pagans. He gets his living by making greegrees, amulets, &c., and selling them to the poor deluded creatures, who are greatly influenced by him through witchcraft and other devilments. All that I can do, is to look up for help, whence help alone can come, and wait for the moving of the cloud. Bear with me, then, my lord. Delay is not always inaction, and my delay is the result of prudence, not indolence. The bishop desires me to remain in Freetown till after the annual meeting of the Church Missionary Society, on Wednesday, December 5th."

The following are extracts from Mr. Leacock's diary, kept by him under these harassing circum-

INTERVIEW WITH THE SPANISH CONSUL. 123

stances, for the information of the Bishop of Barbados :—

"Nov. 30th. I was called on to-day by two very respectable-looking men of the Eboe tribe, to whom Mr. B. has mentioned my readiness to go up with them to their country on the Niger. You cannot imagine the delight which overspread their countenances when they first addressed me, nor the disappointment they suffered when told that there were no means of transportation. It is a great disappointment to me as well as to them. People in the West Indies have no idea of travelling in Africa; and you must bear this in mind, *I am subject to the control of the bishop.*

"Dec. 1st. Another station is suggested, and what sort of one is it? An abandoned outpost of the Church Missionary Society, at which her missionaries laboured for eight years without the least success, and gave it up more than fifteen years since in despair.

"Dec. 3d. I had a singular visit this afternoon from the Spanish Consul, a handsome, dashing fellow, covered with civic or military honours. He made some inquiry about the place of my destination, said he had heard of me through some newspapers, and hoped that the mission which had taken me from my native country would prosper. I thanked him, and said I had been detained here by the desire of the bishop, but that I should be at liberty after Wednesday to leave Sierra Leone in the first vessel which sailed hence for the Gallinas. He then said there

124   INTERVIEW WITH THE SPANISH CONSUL.

was a good opening in *Fernando Po*, and he thought if I had not decided on any particular place, it would be as well to take it into consideration. I told him I dared not think of it, because his government would not countenance any mission not Roman Catholic, seeing that it had already expelled a mission which had been some years there. He said, 'They were Baptist missionaries, and I ordered them from the island for speaking in a public manner disrespectfully of my sovereign, and also for having the audacity to say that in a short time they would drive every Spaniard into the sea. I then considered it high time to drive *them* out, and so gave them twelve months to leave. But a mission from your Church would be as acceptable to me as one from my own Church, seeing there are over nine hundred Protestants in the town who speak as good English as any one in this place.' He then recommended me to obtain through the English gov ernment a promise of protection from the Spanish government; and 'it is more than probable,' said he, ' if you decide on going to Fernando Po, that I will go with you.'"

This interview with the Spaniard encouraged Mr. Leacock to hope that a door of usefulness was about to be opened to him. But Providence had his own purposes of mercy towards the Pongas country, and the old chief Wilkinson, who had now been praying for a missionary through more than twenty years. Ob- stacles soon appeared in the way of a mission to Fer- nando Po, reminding us that when " the man of Mace- donia" was about to appear to St. Paul, the Spirit suf-

MEETING OF THE CHURCH MISSIONARY SOCIETY. 125

fered him not to go into Bithynia. The bishop discouraged the scheme, and still advised Mr. Leacock to examine the Sherbro' Island and the neighbouring part of the continent called Gallinas. This he purposed to do at the first opportunity.

On the 4th of December Mr. Leacock attended a meeting of the assembled Church missionaries. The heat was very oppressive and enervating. In the evening the bishop preached, and alluded to the future conversion through the Church Missionary Society, of the country through which the Niger and the Chadda roll their waters. On the following evening the public missionary meeting took place, at seven o'clock, in Christ-Church, Freetown, the governor presiding. The secretary stated that a wide field was open to missionaries below and above the junction of the Niger and Chadda, and that the Church Missionary Society was prepared to occupy it as soon as the river should be open.

Mr. Leacock having been invited to move the third resolution, was introduced to the meeting by his good friend the governor, who said, "This reverend gentleman has come to us with authority from the Church in the West Indies to open a mission on some part of the western coast of Africa. He is highly recommended by my old friend, Sir W. Colebrooke, governor of the island of Barbados." The common people received Mr. Leacock with a shout which he vainly endeavoured to check. He then proceeded with the address given in the following chapter as recorded in a Sierra Leone newspaper, "The African," of December 13th, 1855.

CHAPTER VIII.

When the Episcopate is a Blessing, and when the Reverse. Value of the Episcopate to Sierra Leone. Its Benefits in the West Indies. Rise of the West Indian Church in consequence of the Episcopate. Establishment of the West Indian Mission. Episcopacy acknowledged by Christendom. Greeting to the Bishop of Sierra Leone. Prophetic declaration.

"Your Excellency, Right Rev. Sir, and my Christian friends,

"The resolution which I have in hand involves very properly one of the most pleasing and delightful of all Christian duties, and consequently meets the full concurrence of my mind and my heart. It is thus expressed:—

"'That this meeting cannot but view the improved financial position of the Church Missionary Society during a year of unexampled pressure and difficulty, occasioned by the war with Russia, together with the happy appointment at this juncture of the right Reverend Dr. Weeks to this diocese, as manifest tokens of the Divine favour towards the great work of evangelizing the heathen, and for these mercies would unite in ascriptions of praise and thanksgiving to the great Head of the Church.'

AND WHEN THE REVERSE.

"My friends, to thank God for all his dispensations towards us, even for such as are most contrary to flesh and blood, is a duty which the Christian who has 'tasted and seen that the Lord is good,' feels incumbent on him, and which, trusting that God is too wise to err, and too good to afflict unnecessarily, he is ready and willing at all times to fulfil. Now, if it be so with respect to dispensations of an afflictive character, how much more ready should he be to praise God for blessings which are congenial with his sanctified feelings and desires, and which seem to be clear and unmistakable evidences of the Divine favour. And will it not be admitted that the mercies referred to in the resolution come under this category? Observe, there are two : the improved condition of your Society's revenue ; and the appointment of a bishop for the diocese.

"With repect to the former, we know indeed that the gift of riches is not always an evidence of the Divine favour ; and as to the latter, experience and observation prove, that the Episcopate, as well as the other orders of the Christian ministry, is a blessing only in proportion as it approaches the high and holy standard of the Gospel. Where it is exercised in a capricious and arbitrary manner to serve selfish or party purposes—to gratify the lust of power, and the promptings and goadings of pride and ambition—where it seeks not to extend the benign and humbling influence of our holy religion, to strengthen the bond of peace, and to promote throughout the whole body unity of spirit, and righteousness of life, it is not a blessing: it is a *curse.*

"But, Christian friends, we trust and hope that in neither of the cases before us have we any reason to anticipate evil. Although I have no personal interest in the prosperity of your Society, not having any connexion with it, yet it is gratifying to me to contemplate its flourishing condition, and the truly Christian spirit, which, under the Divine influence, has made it so.

"And why shall not the same power, which has blessed it with an increase of worldly wealth, direct and overrule the application of that wealth, and render it subservient to the furtherance of the Gospel, and the advancement of God's glory? Why shall not the same grace which has provided the means, regulate, and order, and bless, the appropriation of them?

"Evidently the prosperous condition of your Society's funds, must, at this juncture, in a special manner, be ascribed to the influence of God's grace. At a time when the nation is suffering the bitter effects of one of the most grievous wars that ever scourged a people—at a time when the expenses of this war are felt in every part of the empire, narrowing the comforts of the rich, and augmenting the miseries of the poor—at a time when thousands are weeping over the unconsecrated graves of their slain, with nothing, in numerous instances, to alleviate their sorrows but the shadowy glory which military virtue sheds around the sepulchre of the brave:—at such a time, in the midst of such privation and affliction, we might reasonably enough apprehend a great defalcation in missionary funds. But it is not so. Behold the people humbling themselves before the God of the armies of heaven and earth,—hear them declare that He is worthy to receive *all riches*, as well as honour and glory—see them actually give their riches—give what they acknowledge He is so worthy to receive—give what they can spare, to advance in the heathen world the glory and honour of his holy Name. Surely, this is God's doing; and might it not reasonably lead us to hope that a work so begun—begun in humiliation and prayer, and having such an end in view, *God's glory*, will be carried on in the same spirit till finally its desired consummation be attained? This, Christian friends, is one of the mercies for which we are called upon in the resolution to render unto God devout thanksgiving and praise.

"With respect to the other mercy referred to in the resolution, viz., the consecration of a bishop for this diocese, I cannot say much, for a reason which must appear to every delicate and sensible mind. But, though a sense of decency, and respect for an honoured individual, check the language of praise, we must not pass by his office in absolute silence.

"For the appointment of a bishop to this Church, you ought indeed to rejoice and be glad; and, in this instance, I have great satisfaction in obeying the apostolic injunction, 'Rejoice with them that do rejoice.' Episcopalians have, from time to time, been subjected to the contradiction and ridicule of their opponents, because of this distinctive feature in their Church

6*

government; but, waiving every remark respecting its origin, I feel pleasure in saying that whatever may be my opinion of certain bishops, I have never seen any just reason to be ashamed of Episcopacy; on the contrary, I have seen much cause for thankfulness for it.

"It was my lot to reside in one of the West Indian islands, some thirty years, previous to their connexion by the Episcopal form of Christian government: and I well remember the looseness and irregularity which prevailed under so dislocated a state of the Church. There was no visible head to unite and direct the movements of the Clergy—none to whom they were responsible; and the consequence was that each and every rector acted independently of his brother rectors, and was *de facto*, if not *de jure*, a little bishop in his little diocese. He acted just as he pleased, and gave account to no man for his actions. You may easily imagine the working or operation of so defective a system upon the world. The watchmen were many of them 'dumb dogs that could not bark;' and 'the people loved to have it so.' Duties, in many instances, were neglected, or most irreverently performed; and the West Indian Church exhibited a counterpart of Israel of old, 'where,' says the sacred historian, 'there was no king, and every man did that which was right in his own eyes.'

"But no sooner did a bishop appear amongst us than his authority was recognized. The Church suddenly arose as from a state of death, and assumed the appearance of a well-ordered, compact body. Its dis-

RISE OF THE WEST INDIAN CHURCH. 131

cipline was instantly established. Its ministers began
to remember themselves. Its services were regularly
and more reverently performed. The stillness of death
suddenly diappeared, and was succeeded by a busy,
bustling religion, which, if it had not life, had at least
the appearance of it. After a while, under the wise
and judicious administration of our bishop, every obstacle to order and unity was removed; and the
Church began to take her proper stand, and to gather
and to bless her children, and, by her reflex influence,
to bless and enrich *even those who refused to own her
authority*. Yes, Christian friends, our dissenting
brethren felt the salutary change, and thankfully acknowledged it. ' Our work,' said one of them to me,
' our work flourishes most when there is a stirring, faithful, devoted ministry in the parish church ; for then
our unruly members, who leave us to go into the Establishment, cannot be easy when they hear the same
awakening truths, the same awful sanctions both of
Law and Gospel, which offended them in our chapel ;
and they are compelled to cast away their empty profession of religion, and return to our chapel, or become consistent members of the Establishment.'

"Such was the effect, by God's blessing, of Episcopacy in the West Indies. The Church has continued to grow and increase under its influences, till,
strengthened at home, she is now making efforts to
send abroad, to distant heathen nations, the savour of
that name, which, as sweet ointment, is poured forth
within her own borders.

"At a meeting of our Barbados Church Society

132   ESTABLISHMENT OF THE MISSION.

in 1850, a proposition was made to open a mission for
the furtherance of the Gospel on the western coast of
Africa. The proposition was hailed with joy, and
carried by acclamation, not one *appearing* in opposition to it. That part of our population which is of
African descent rejoiced at the thought of sending to
some benighted portion of their fatherland the glad
tidings of salvation, and presently a considerable sum
of money was raised for the purpose.

"But this excitement was not of long duration.
The people of every class and description soon became
discouraged, on account of what they deemed culpa-
ble delay; for year after year passed away, and no
one could be found in a position to undertake the work,
till it pleased the great Head of the Church to put into
the mind of an humble individual, then an acting
member of the association, a desire to visit this country, and report what prospect of success there appeared
for the establishment of such a mission. That individual's proposal was accepted immediately by the bishop
and the committee of the association, and he received
forthwith his appointment as missionary to the western coast of Africa. He left the West Indies on the
15th day of July; and here he is, having the honour
now to stand before you, and to address you.

"Christian friends, the West Indian Church has
learned by experience to appreciate duly the blessing
of Episcopacy; and when about to open her mission,
though she would not intrude in the labours of other
men, or build upon their foundation—though she desire to send the Gospel afar off to a people sitting in

EPISCOPACY ACKNOWLEDGED BY CHRISTENDOM. 133

darkness, not having the lamp of life amongst them, yet she will not neglect or exclude from her mission the advantages of Episcopacy when they can be obtained.

" She sends that mission to your land, not invested with any independent or exclusive power. She commits it, under the Great Bishop of souls, to the oversight of the Bishop of Sierra Leone, confiding in his generous, impartial, affectionate, fostering care. She commits it to the supervision of your bishop, not (let me be distinctly understood) because she has no confidence in the prudence, faithfulness, or integrity of her deputation; for if she had intimated such a thought, you would never have seen me here. She commends her mission to the care of your bishop, because she recognizes in his office a something superior to the ordinance of man, and would honour it as a form of ecclesiastical government ' most agreeable with the institution of Christ.'

" It is remarkable that this form of Church government, Episcopacy, seems to have the consent of Christendom. The English Church; the Eastern and Western, or the Greek and Roman Churches; the Coptic, Abyssinian, and Armenian Churches, all have bishops. Even our dissenting brethren, the Wesleyans, have in the United States what they actually call ' The Methodist Episcopal Church ;' and the other branches of that society have forms of government very analogous to ours. Though they recognize as stewards of the mysteries of the Gospel only such as can distinctly and unequivocally declare that they are called and

134 GREETING TO THE BISHOP OF SIERRA LEONE.

sent by the Holy Ghost, yet they see the wisdom and
necessity of setting apart in every district under their
influence one as superintendent of the district. They
do not call this *Episcopacy*, as do their American
brethren, and they are certainly correct, but it is something very like it; and they are fully convinced that
without such a form of government, anarchy would
soon pervade and disorganize the whole fabric of their
well-consolidated system.

"And now, your Excellency, and Christian friends,
shall we not admit that the privilege of Episcopacy,
as well as the improvement of your Society's finances,
calls for our acknowledgment and thanksgiving? I
trust you are all sensible of its importance as a privilege; and I hope the time is not far distant, when
the Church in Sierra Leone will come forth, resplen-
dent in Christian graces, strong in the strength of
Omnipotence, and not only sustain itself independently of the fostering care of the Church Missionary Society, but follow its example, in training the youth of
Africa for the work of the ministry; and that she
will send them forth, *at her own charge*, to proclaim
the glad tidings of salvation in the far east, and south,
and north,—far beyond the Kong mountains, into the
kingdoms of darkness and cruelty which crowd the
interior of this widely extended and mighty continent.

"I beg, therefore, most heartily to congratulate
you, my brethren of this diocese, and to be permitted
to unite with you in ascriptions of praise and thanksgiving to the great Head of the Church, for the im-

PROPHETIC DECLARATION. 135

provement of the financial concerns of your Society; and for the appointment of a gentleman to preside over this portion of the Lord's vineyard as bishop, who is so acceptable to you, whose views of Christian doctrine so entirely accord with your own, and whose experience, wisdom, and Christian character, encourage us to hope that peace shall dwell within our border, and that the Lord has yet in store *good things* for poor, degraded, benighted, bleeding Africa.

"Right Rev. Sir, in the name of the West Indian Church, which I have the honour. to represent here this evening, I *bid you God's speed.* It is a frequent subject of my prayers; and I shall cease to pray for it when I cease to stand in need of prayer for myself. The world, Sir, is witnessing great events, and the future is pregnant with greater still.

"That general promise which the Father hath made to the Son, 'Ask of me, and I shall give thee the heathen for thine inheritance, and the uttermost parts of the earth for thy possession,' must in due time be fully realized; but, Sir, there is a particular promise on record for our encouragement, which I pray it may be our happy lot, before we go hence, to behold in a course of rapid fulfilment.

"It is that great event to which the English Church in general, and your Society in particular, are looking forward with 'earnest expectation'—that prophetic declaration of the inspired volume, which stands firmer than the mountains, and as firm as the foundations of high heaven: 'Ethiopia shall soon stretch out her hands unto God.'"

CHAPTER IX.

Melville Horne on the Qualifications of an African Missionary. The Rio Pongas is mentioned to Mr. Leacock. The Governor promises to send Mr. Leacock to the Pongas in a Steamer. Character of Governor Hill. Meeting with a Mohammedan King. Landing at Tintima. Palaver with Kennyback Ali and King Katty. Description of the Pongas River. Hut at Tintima. Wretched character of the people. Deceitfulness of Kennyback Ali. Mr. Leacock visits him. Encounter with a Mohammedan.

THE time had now come when the long-continued prayers of the Chief Wilkinson were to receive a gracious answer. A missionary indeed was to be sent to him,—not a missionary of the Church of Rome, nor of any separated community, but a missionary of the reformed Church of England,—full of earnest zeal for the salvation of men, devoted to the cause of Africa, abundant in prayer, in faith, in hope, and in charity.

The Rev. Melville Horne, chaplain at Sierra Leone in the early part of this century, published a valuable little book on African missions, from which the following extracts are here inserted, with the view of showing Mr. Leacock's fitness for the work which he had undertaken :—

HORNE ON MISSIONARY QUALIFICATIONS. 137

" Piety is the only basis of the missionary character; but a tolerable strength and maturity of religion will be as needful as the sincerity of it. Zeal is a qualification of a nature inferior only to piety, and that man will hardly be defective in it who enters upon missions in compliance with the bent of his own inclinations. It is to be wished that the missionary's zeal should not have been lately kindled, but such as having burned for years, promises to continue in its heat. His fire should be moderated by some experience in the ministry. He should have been taught to exercise a good degree of gentleness, patience, and long-sufferance, by being accustomed to wrestle with the unruly will of men, by seeing many of his well-meant efforts frustrated through invincible depravity, and by observing the failure of some of his most sanguine and reasonable expectations. There is an art in managing men's minds which nothing but experience can teach. That man will have little skill in ruling the tempest of the human passions, who has not learned to moderate the ardour of his own feelings, and who does not know when to press his point and when to decline it,—when to command and when to entreat.

" There are some pious men who are capable of every thing, and yet do very little in life. They are disorderly in all their habits and versatile in all their pursuits. Superior to fear, they are, unhappily, ductile, and receive the impression of minds inferior to their own. Capable of vast exertions, they are naturally indolent. With a vivacity which often sparkles and charms, they unite a morbid melancholy which preys upon the heart. They are amiable, but not venerable. Such men may engage in missions, but will hardly succeed in them.

"The missionary should possess much self-denial, and be regular in all his habits. He need not have the razor's edge; but he must be as the blade of a well-tempered knife. He must be a man of discipline and self-command.

"His character should be divested of sloth, effeminacy, and indulgence. Perhaps he should rather be *capable* of becoming a man of letters than actually be so. All his habits should be active rather than sedentary. A disposition favourable to the feelings of ardent and sublime devotion, and a delight in the exercises of the pulpit and the pastoral care, should preponderate in his character. In a word, he should be more the active man than the contemplative one. A sound constitution, hardèned to the vicissitudes of the seasons, and capable of supporting the extremes of suffering, is greatly to be desired; but a mind superior to suffering is a consideration of far more importance than that corporeal vigour and hardness which is invulnerable to fatigue and want.

"We require in our missionary a disinterested, generous way of thinking and acting, above low cunning, servile compliance, and a presumptuous invasion of powers to which his character does not entitle him. We would have him sincere, open, and affectionate. Instead of authoritative commands, we would arm him with prayers, entreaties, and tears.

FIRST MENTION OF THE PONGAS.

We expect that he should have learned to bear and forbear. We think that ignorance should excite his pity, and not rouse his contempt. He *must* be an extempore preacher, and possess a facility of conveying to the mind his ideas clear and strong, independently of those modes of speech which originate in the laws and manners of Europe.

"Single men are the proper persons for this work; they have no ties. Private charities will not counteract public ones. They can live cheap, fare hard, and are ready for every service. If they have the souls of missionaries in them, they will often, between their charity and their zeal, be placed in circumstances similar to those of St. Paul,—in nakedness, in want, in perils by land, in perils by sea, and in all the varieties of suffering."

Soon after the missionary meeting in Freetown, Mr. Galbridden, a merchant trading with the Pongas, in conversation with Mr. Leacock, spoke of the inhabitants of that country as presenting an open field to Christian exertions. Mr. Leacock went immediately to the governor, who, as well as the bishop, thought it worthy of further notice. Dining with the governor on the 7th, he mentioned to Mrs. Hill his intention of going to the Pongas, in an open canoe, along a hundred and forty miles of coast. The governor's lady referred him for information to Captain Buck, of Her Majesty's steamer "Myrmidon," who was at that moment seated at the table. The captain, who had just arrived from the Pongas, informed Mr. Leacock that there would be danger in travelling in an open canoe, which would expose him to alternate damp and heat during four nights and as many days, in addition to the usual risks of the sea. "But," said he, " if you like it, I will take you there in one day, and wait two days for you, that you may have an interview with some of the chiefs; but you must have the consent of the governor." "Thank you, my dear captain," replied Mr. Leacock, " if it depend on the governor's consent I shall have it, I know." Accordingly he spoke across the table to the governor:— " Colonel, here is an open way before me, if you do not bar it up." On being informed of his wish, the governor replied, "The captain has my consent with all my heart and soul."

Mr. Leacock described to the Bishop of Barbados what followed. " Of course," he writes, " I thankfully accepted this gracious offer; and so, if no obstacle arise, I shall embark the day after to-morrow, Monday. This will save our association about fifteen pounds at least. If I am well received, I shall select a location at once, and return for my baggage."

" Dec. 8th. I have just seen Mr. Galbridden, who seems to rejoice in the good prospects for the Pongas people, and volunteers to go with me, that he may introduce me to the people, and provide a lodgement for me in this wild wilderness. It is emphatically missionary ground,—it has never been broken; the Gospel has never been sounded there. I have been baffled hitherto in every attempt, and so I am afraid to say how or in what way this new scheme will issue; but I do not despair. This letter I shall leave with my friend Mr. Pocock, as I fear I shall not return in time for the packet. If it should leave before my return, you may be assured that I have gone to the Pongas in the steamer 'Myrmidon;' and it would be well, perhaps, if your lordship would write to the Secretary for the Colonies, and express to him our hearty thanks for the great assistance I have received from Governor Hill and Captain Buck. Governor Hill is a prompt, active, diligent official, very much loved here, and deservedly so; for his great object seems to be to promote the happiness, spiritual and temporal, of the people over whom he is placed. May the Lord bless him abundantly for his kindness to me. I think an acknowledgment to the Secretary of his kindness is our duty, as no doubt it will be satisfactory to him to know how greatly his influence has helped us.

"I am invited to luncheon to-day at Government House, to meet a magnificent Mohammedan king, and to dine this evening with the Honourable the Chief Justice. I am whirled in a round of dissipation, and shall be more than glad of a little quiet duty in the Pongas."

On Monday, Dec. 10th, the "Myrmidon" left Freetown with Mr. Leacock and Duport on board. The reader will no doubt agree with the writer in thinking that a British ship of war was never better employed than in thus forwarding the Gospel of the Prince of Peace. In conversation on the way, Captain Buck plainly set before Mr. Leacock the peril which he was incurring in venturing on a residence in the

142 A MOHAMMEDAN KING.

Pongas. The missionary, however, was moved by no such consideration. After a rapid voyage along the coast towards the N.N.W., they arrived at the mouth of the river on Tuesday, the 11th. The following letter to Governor Hill, written by Mr. Leacock on board the "Myrmidon," on the 15th, describes the first interview of the missionary with the people of the country :—

" We came to an anchorage off the mouth of the Rio Pongas on Tuesday, the 11th instant, ten miles outside of the bar ; and it being too late for the tide, we had to wait till next morning, when, in two boats, well manned and armed, we commenced our journey at eight o'clock up the river, and arrived at Tintima, the residence of the renowned Kennyback Ali, at about three P.M. I say *about*, for, as it happened, no one had his watch with him ; each supposing that his would be far safer in the 'Myrmidon' than in Tintima, exposed to the gaze of our distinguished host and his myrmidons.

" We were soon ushered into the presence of the chief, although we anticipated nought but delay, on account of his health, which is delicate, and which renders an occasional visit in the country necessary. The captain requested me to appear in my gown ; and supported by him on one hand, and Captain Fletcher, of the 1st West India Regiment, on the other, both in uniform, I was introduced to the noble chief. In long, loose, flowing robes, gracefully descending to his naked and unadorned feet, and head crowned with a Kilmarnock cap, he met us, and re-

PALAVER WITH THE KINGS. 143

ceived us with every mark of respect. He invited us
into the piazza of one of his amplest buildings, and
desired us to be seated. Then, after very friendly
inquiries respecting your Excellency's health, he
wished to know our business—wished to 'sabby
whether our visit was for war-palaver.' *Our* chief
replied, with extraordinary gravity, ' No, your
Majesty : our visit is altogether friendly, and has
for its object the consolidation and advancement of
peace.' (Of course we had an interpreter.) He then
introduced me as an instrument intended to carry
this design into effect. He told him of my profession, explained whence I had come, and the object
of my coming, and stated that Her Britannic Majesty's Government highly approved of my mission,
and requested him to afford me protection and encouragement in the work on which I was sent. The man
eyed me in my length and breadth, and, as we afterwards heard, had some suspicion of the character of
my mission, supposing that it bore upon the slave
trade ; but soon he replied, ' Yease, me like him, me
like him; but nutting to-day, nutting to-day ; to-morrow palaver, when de king come.'

"Instantly an order was issued to man a canoe,
and take advantage of the tide. The captain, in full
uniform, seemed to command the greatest respect ;
but the mention of the governor of Sierra Leone, and
especially of our beloved Victoria, acted like a charm.
The next day, at 11 o'clock A.M., a herald from the
river-side announced the arrival of Matthias Katty,
king of the Pongas, accompanied by his suite ; and

to his sable majesty, in the course of an hour, I had the honour of a formal introduction. He was evidently prepared for the subject of the palaver; and when the letter of Her Majesty's representative was put into his hand, he seemed greatly elevated by it, and said, ' Yease, me gib my children to de ould man to teach dem ; but a—a—'

"The great difficulty which operated against us, was the idea that I required him and all his subjects to submit to my instruction, which the crafty monarch too well knew would reduce the number of inmates in his harem to a solitary unit. *This* no earthly power could induce him to do ; and, therefore, he urged that he and his 'big people' wanted no teaching, but the children wanted it, and he would send *his* directly if the Queen would clothe them. The captain explained that no one would be compelled to attend the ministry of Mr. Leacock; but he hoped he, the king, would not prevent such as were disposed. This satisfied him.

"Soon after, eight chiefs, great landholders, appeared, and demanded a private palaver with the two kings. They caused us some difficulty, and for a time shook the dicision of the kings. Things now seemed desperate, and nothing was expected by us but an immediate return to Sierra Leone. The eight chiefs were Mandingoes, professed Mohammedans, and, of course, bitterly opposed to Christianity. The kings not yielding to them, they desired five days to consider the matter. This, however, was a mere manœuvre, as I learned from my assistant, John Duport, to whom

PALAVER WITH THE KINGS. 145

it was hinted that no presents were given to the Mandingoes. The cunning fellows desired to take advantage of an Englishman's promptness in doing business, and his impatience of delay, and therefore demanded such a time for consideration as they knew we should be unwilling to give, and hoped to compromise the matter by receiving a handsome present from us. I knew that yielding to such a desire would only increase their wretched appetite, and entail upon me interminable demands. It was Captain Buck's opinion also, and he united with me in the objection. I said, in the presence of them all, ' It has been hinted to me that the eight chiefs desire presents to induce them to come at once to a favourable decision. Now, I will begin as I intend to end. It is not my intention to offer any present, neither at this time nor at any other. I have not come to trade with them, nor to ask of them any favour, but to do them good, if possible ; therefore, the obligation is on their part, not on mine ; and if presents are to be given, *I* am the person to *re ceive*. But I give them all I have, *myself*, and I ask nothing in return but *themselves*, that is, a desire on their part to benefit by my presence and teaching. All I have I give, I trust, in the spirit and feeling of an Apostle, who, upon being asked for alms, replied, ' Silver and gold have I none, but such as I have give I unto thee.' If I can be instrumental in bringing them to the great Physician of souls, to heal their spiritual diseases, it is all I can do for them. If they choose to receive me with such intentions, here I am, willing to remain with them ; if not, brethren, say at

7

once, and we will be off next tide to Sierra Leone.'
This had the desired effect. The Mandingoes sneaked
away, and King Katty said to Captain Buck, 'We
take um—we glad to hab um.'

After the palaver was at an end, I said to Katty
in a private conversation, Captain Buck only being
present, 'King Katty, I am come to you in God's
name, to do you and your people good. I shall soon
be alone with you. My friends, who have come to
protect me, will soon leave me, and I shall be then
entirely at your mercy. Nevertheless, I am not afraid
of *you* nor of your Mandingoes. You can do with me
what you please. I am not afraid to die, whether it
be by fever or by sword. I am come with a message
of mercy to you and your people; if you reject me
and cut me off, I do not refuse to die—it will be
better for me, for then I shall go home,' lifting up my
right hand, and looking upwards.

" How astonished was I, as well as Captain Buck,
to hear this untutored savage's prompt reply,—'Aye,
yease; but if we reject you and send you off, de gret
God will reject we and cut we off.' I replied, 'Certainly, most certainly.'

" Your Excellency is aware that both Kennybeck
Ali and Matthias Katty speak a little English, and
can understand an Englishman condescending to speak
in their 'fashin.' Soon every thing was arranged.
King Katty signed a declaration (drawn up hastily and
in the last moment, intended for your Excellency),
and then we separated. King Katty returned to his
friends, and right early next morning, as soon as the

tide permitted, we took our boats, and in seven hours reached the ' Myrmidon.'

"I cannot thank your Excellency too much for committing the management of this affair to Captain Buck. His gentlemanly and kind attention to me is such as might be expected of one in his responsible position. His influence over the savage people of the Pongas seems to be very great, and his diplomatic tact very efficacious. It has secured for me not only a respectful, but a friendly reception amongst them. Kennyback Ali received and entertained us all very hospitably, and offered me the use of one of his houses until I could be better provided for. King Katty said he would build a house for me, and give me a piece of ground for a garden, &c., but I know not how much dependence is to be placed on his word. Even if he duly conform to his promise, it will afford me very little accommodation; for the houses, built of mud walls, or wattled and dabbed, consist of only one room, and that a circular one, without windows, but with two doors opposite to each other, and afford no privacy, no security, no comfort, but shelter only. This, however, I shall be thankful for, when I get it; and shall continue to trust that same good Providence which has hitherto been with me, and which will continue to follow me."

On Monday, the 17th, Mr. Leacock and Duport left their friends in the "Myrmidon," and again proceeded up the Little Pongas to Tintima, relying on the promises of Kennyback Ali and King Katty. Their means of conveyance was a narrow canoe, which appeared far from safe. An upset would be followed by almost certain destruction. If a person thus situated were to escape the sharks, a rapid tide would be likely to drown him; if by any chance he were to reach the river's bank, he would sink in the soft mud; and if he escaped the mud, he would probably be devoured in the jungle by wild beasts. Alligators conceal themselves in the rank vegetation which borders this beautiful river, and which is so interlaced that, once in it, there is no egress without brawny shoulders and a faithful broad axe.

Geographers have taken little notice of this river, and it merits greater attention than it has yet received. It rises probably in the Kong mountains. It is navigable for small craft about twenty miles, and in some places is full three quarters of a mile in breadth. The mouth, where, with the Big Pongas, it enters the sea, is more than two miles broad, but is dangerous to vessels by reason of a sand-bar, over which the sea breaks at all times with great violence, except in a narrow channel on the north side, which is not quite safe to pass even at high tide. As I have already mentioned in the sixth chapter, Tintima is situated on the Little Pongas, about nine miles above the bar.

On arriving at Tintima, Mr. Leacock and Duport took possession of a wretched cone-shaped hut, which had been awarded to them by Kennyback Ali, according to agreement. They now had an opportunity of examining the village rather more closely than during their visit of the preceding week.

They found Tintima very similar to the large ne-

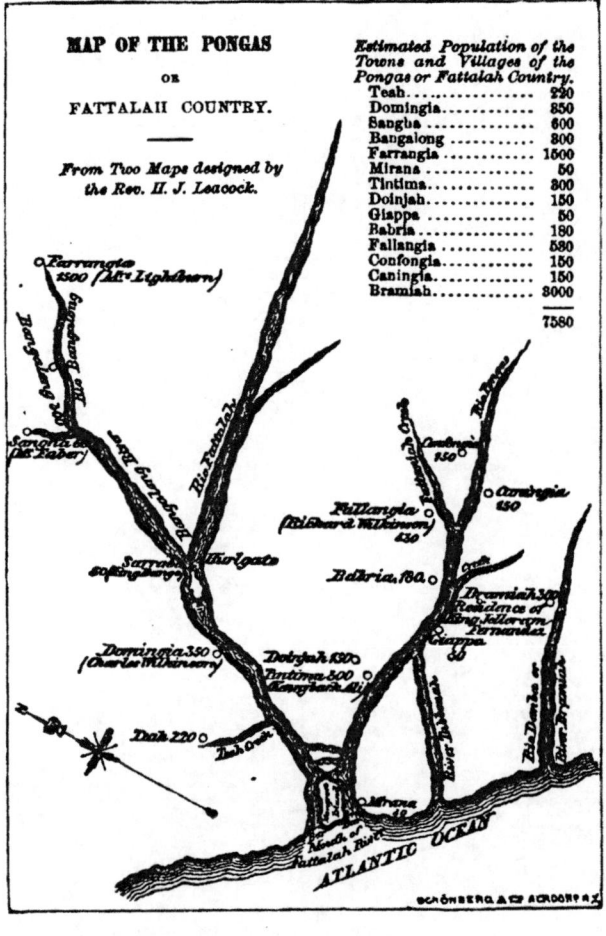

MAP OF THE PONGAS

OR

FATTALAH COUNTRY.

From Two Maps designed by
the Rev. H. J. Leacock.

Estimated Population of the Towns and Villages of the Pongas or Fattalah Country.	
Teah	220
Domingia	350
Sangba	600
Bangalong	800
Farrangia	1500
Mirana	50
Tintima	300
Doinjah	150
Giappa	50
Babria	180
Fallangia	580
Confongia	150
Caningia	150
Bramiah	3000
	7580

WRETCHED CHARACTER OF THE PEOPLE. 151

gro villages which existed in the West Indies during
the days of slavery. There was no street, but the
houses appeared as if scattered. They were placed
in this irregular manner purposely to avoid the observation of an enemy attacking them suddenly in the
night. The cottages were all miserable affairs, having only one room, generally circular, but sometimes
square. The inside of the roof always had a very
filthy appearance, having long cobwebs descending,
and black from the smoke of a fire made in the centre
of the room to destroy insects harboured in the roof.
In such a house the missionaries were for the present
established. It was quite open, without a lock to
either of the doors, and the men and women of the
village were constantly coming in (*in puris naturali-
bus*) and carrying off with their nimble fingers whatever was left outside of the trunks and boxes. Mr.
Leacock and Duport were compelled to keep watch
alternately, to save themselves from being thoroughly
plundered.

The reception which they had met with from
Kennyback Ali in the presence of Captains Buck and
Fletcher had been kind enough; but now that the
" Myrmidon " had departed they were left entirely at
the mercy of his slaves. Cheated and peeled as these
people had been by traders, they did not forget to be
avenged on the strangers. Provisions were withheld,
with the object of extortion, and Mr. Leacock and
his companion would have gone without food on the
day of their arrival, had they not found in one of
their boxes a jar of preserved ginger. They ate the

152 WRETCHED CHARACTER OF THE PEOPLE.

ginger with some biscuits which they had fortunately brought from the "Myrmidon," and drank the syrup mixed with water, after which they finished their repast with water, cup after cup, till they were satisfied. They asked for fowls, usually sold at four or five shillings a dozen, but now one fowl was offered for two shillings. They asked for eggs, which are sold at a half-penny each ; a dollar was now asked for twenty. After finding that the missionaries had a supply of biscuit, the natives began to lower their demands. No servant was, however, to be procured, so that they were obliged to wait on themselves. Fortunately they found a woman from Sierra Leone who could wash clothes, but as there was no smoothing iron in the place, they were compelled to wear their clothes rough dried. Duport was at first much discouraged, but he soon recovered himself, and bore his privations without a murmur, believing that this would be a good discipline, and a preparation for future scenes. Kennyback Ali had twenty wives, and religious principles which could be readily accommodated to Mohammedanism, heathenism, or any other doctrine. His pretended support to Christianity, therefore, probably originated in the pension awarded him by the British Government for abandoning the slave trade himself, and for engaging to check it in others. All the country was laid waste by wars instigated by slavers. Slaves were still brought from the interior, and stealthily shipped in the river. But for the fear of British ships there would be no check upon the trade. There were barracoons still concealed in va-

A COTTAGE IN TINTIMA, PONGAS COUNTRY,

Occupied by the Rev. H. J. Leacock and Mr. Duport, Dec. 18, 1855, from
a sketch by Mr. Leacock. The roof is of grass.

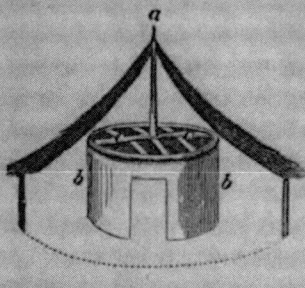

Interior Structure of the Cottage.

a. pole supporting the top of the
    roof.
b b. wall.
c c. pieces of wood thrown across
    the wall, supporting the pole.

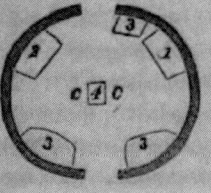

Plan of the Interior of the Cottage.

1. Mr. Leacock's lodging.
2. Mr. Duport's.
3 3 3. baggage.
4. table.
c c. chairs. No window.

154   VISIT TO KENNYBACK ALI.

rious places, for slavers have many stratagems to escape the vigilance of our steamers. Kennyback Ali told Mr. Leacock that he owned many slaves himself, and had no objection to sell them if they were to go into the interior.

Kennyback Ali being at this time confined to his bed by illness at Doinjah, a village three miles from Tintima, Mr. Leacock walked out to see him on the 19th of December, leaving Duport to guard the house. The track lay partly through high grass, and partly through wood, the vegetation on every side being thick and rank. The guide informed Mr. Leacock that the *boa constrictor* was found every where throughout the neighbourhood, and that the place through which they were passing was infested with venomous snakes. Deer also and wild cattle, tiger-cats and leopards, were often seen there. It was Mr. Leacock's first walk through an African forest, which he found very different from the forests in Tennessee, through which he had travelled with good Bishop Otey.

On arriving at the sick man's house, he found him lying on a hammock, surrounded by eight of his friends, apparently men of some note. He took the opportunity of addressing them on the subject of his mission, and mentioned salvation through Christ. It happened that one of them spoke English sufficiently to act as interpreter. Most of them seemed little moved by what was said. The sick man appeared to be a little interested, and rose and sat across his hammock when Mr. Leacock began to speak. No one,

VISIT TO KENNYBACK ALI.   155

however, said any thing in reply, beyond expressing
surprise on hearing that some of their negro brethren
in the West Indies had assisted in sending the missionaries.

Mr. Leacock returned through the wood with perfect serenity, notwithstanding the information which
he had received respecting its dangerous inhabitants.
But every succeeding day showed him that his prospects in Tintima were almost hopeless. The conduct
of the people became more and more discouraging,
for they said that the missionaries had been sent by
the British Government to interfere with their slaves.
It was evident that the poor wretch, Kennyback Ali,
would not say, " You must leave us," from the fear
of losing his pension ; but his actions and the actions
of his people spoke out too plainly to be misunderstood. Children were promised Mr. Leacock as
pupils ; but not a single child was actually sent. Two
boys were constantly lounging about the house, and
John Duport accordingly began to teach them their
letters. But they were immediately ordered to "quit
book, and not return to de white man."

About this time Mr. Leacock had a very unsatisfactory encounter with a Mohammedan. He affirmed
that Mohammed was a true prophet ; but when asked
for his credentials, he was silent. Mr. Leacock told
him that Jesus Christ had his credentials, and produced them ; and that if they were necessary to
prove Him true, Mohammed, who had none, must be
false. " Come to-morrow, come to-morrow," said he,
laughing, and went away.

156   EVENTS OF ST. THOMAS'S DAY.

CHAPTER X.

Events of St. Thomas's Day.   Arrival of Lewis Wilkinson.   Interview
with the chief of Fallangia.   Mr. Leacock opens his Ministry among
the Heathens.   Mr. Wilkinson gives him a Site for a Church, &c.   The
Missionaries are attacked with Fever.   Anxiety of Governor Hill on
their Account.   He sends a Steamer and removes them to Sierra Leone.
They return to Fallangia.   John Duport begins to teach.   Supplies ordered in England.

In the midst of these discouragements, Mr. Leacock
continued cheerful and confident that Providence
would at last open a door for the Gospel.   While he
was awaiting the issue of events, St. Thomas's Day,
Dec. 21st, arrived, and a boat was seen descending
the Little Pongas, and approaching Tintima.   On
arriving at the landing place a young black man
stepped ashore and proceeded to the miserable hovel
occupied by the two missionaries.   On meeting Mr.
Leacock, he introduced himself in a most respectful
manner, and speaking excellent English, disclosed the
object of his errand.

"Sir," he said, "my name is Lewis Wilkinson,
and I am a son of Mr. Wilkinson, the chief of Fal-

langia, to whom you forwarded a letter from Mr. Galbridden, of Sierra Leone. I bring an invitation from my father and an apology for his not having called to see you before. He is now very sick, but wishes to know when it will suit you to come to him, that he may send for you." Mr. Leacock was then in a state of great suffering, his hands and face being swollen, and his feet sore from the bites of mosquitoes. His visitor, seeing this, proceeded :—"Sir, my father desires a day or two to make some preparation to receive you, but I cannot leave you in this state. You must go to Fallangia with me this evening, and see whether some better accommodation can be made for you than what you have here, for it is very doubtful whether a stranger can live in this place during the wet season."

Mr. Leacock thankfully accepted the invitation, believing that he saw in it the hand of Providence. Accordingly, leaving Duport to guard the baggage, he accompanied Lewis Wilkinson on board the boat, and the negro rowers conveyed them up the Little Pongas. The following remarkable extract from one of Mr. Leacock's letters describes his first interview with the venerable chief of Fallangia :—

" The old man met me, and taking my hand in both of his hands, pressed it cordially, and, before releasing it, said, ' Welcome, dear Sir, thou servant of the Most High, you are welcome to this humble roof.' I attempted to apologize for having come that evening : he said, ' No apology, Sir: if you will be satisfied with my humble board, you are welcome;' and

158   INTERVIEW WITH THE CHIEF.

he ordered supper immediately. He seemed greatly
agitated, and, a few moments after, rising from his
chair, broke forth with that incomparable song of
praise, the 'Te Deum Laudamus;' repeating it with
great solemnity and accuracy. At the conclusion,
after a short silence, he said : 'Sir, this requires explanation. In my youth I was sent to your country,
and placed under the tuition of a respectable clergyman, and through him I imbibed the first principles
of Christianity. I returned to my native country in
1813, and fell into many of its ungodly practices. In
this state I continued till 1835, when it pleased God
to visit me with severe illness, from which I with difficulty recovered. From that time I resolved that "I
and my house would serve the Lord ;" and I earnestly
prayed that God would send a missionary to this Pongas country, whom I might see before I died. I have
written to Sierra Leone for a missionary, but could
get no answer; and now the Lord has sent me an answer. You are, Sir, an answer to my prayers for
twenty years. You are the first minister of the Gospel I have beheld since 1835. And now I know that
God hears prayer, and that a blessing is come to my
house. Here you are welcome. I know the misery
you must have endured at Tintima, left to the mercy
of those creatures. It is the most unfit place for a
stranger in the Pongas ; and if you resolve on remaining there during the wet season, you are a dead man.
As you have come to our country, I will find plenty
of work for you. The king of this country is Jelloram
Fernandez : I am his cousin ; and my son is married

to one of his daughters. I know all the chiefs; and I will go with you to visit them as soon as I am able. There are in Fallangia over thirty children, which will be the beginning of a school for you. You can use my house; and next fall I will assist you in putting up a house for you to reside in, and a place of worship. In the mean time I will divide my house with you, and not charge you house-rent. You can have a private table, if you prefer it; and if you should be sick, I will help nurse you.'

"Well, well, well, thought I, if this be a true man (and there was too much earnestness in his manner to suppose him false), surely the Lord must have sent me to him, and I have nothing to do but remain."

It is to be observed that when the son of Mr. Wilkinson and old Martha saw Mr. Leacock, he told his parents that he was exactly like the missionary whom he had seen in his dream. Mr. Leacock landed at the same place which the young man had previously indicated.

"On Sunday, the 23rd," proceeds Mr. Leacock, "we had Morning Service in Mr. Wilkinson's piazza, a room 132 feet in length, by 12 feet in breadth, and a room into which it leads 24 feet in breadth. I had it measured. A part of this piazza was pretty well filled by different persons; some understanding a little English. We sang the 100th Psalm, and I preached from the words, 'My son, give me thy heart.' After the service, the old man explained to those who could not understand me the substance of my sermon. All seemed greatly pleased.

"I felt unwell, and retired to rest a little. As soon as I was heard stirring, one who was waiting outside at the door came to me, and said that the congregation was waiting to know whether I would have another sermon before they left. Instantly I obeyed the summons ; and, after a selection of the prayers, and singing a psalm, I preached from the 1st and 2nd verses of the 32nd Psalm, to a serious and attentive little audience. The old man was greatly delighted. Notes are of no use here. Plain, simple exposition of Scripture, and practical application, are all that is necessary. Here then my ministry is fully announced."

Mr. Wilkinson now gave Mr. Leacock a beautiful site for his residence. It was his own garden, comprising about two acres and a half, enclosed with a *physic-nut* fence. It contained a number of orange-trees, mangoes and other fruit-trees. He declared that he should write and specify distinctly that this land was given to the West Indian Church Association, for the use and accommodation of its missionaries, as long as the mission should exist amongst his people; and that, if the mission should be removed, it should revert to him and his heirs.

The next morning, the 24th, Mr. Leacock embarked with the ebb tide, and returned to Tintima for his baggage. He had written to Kennyback Ali on the Saturday, informing him of his intention to leave Tintima, thanking him for the small attentions which he had received, and promising to come to him and open a school when requested to do so. He now called again to see him, walking three miles in the

AN ATTACK OF FEVER. 161

middle of the day, under a broiling sun, through the dangerous forest. He was told, on his arrival, that Kennyback Ali was asleep and would not be disturbed. No one offered him a seat or a cup of cold water. After walking back again, he commenced removing his baggage with the help of Duport and the rowers of the boat, no one coming to their assistance. At a quarter after six on Christmas Eve they left Tintima, and landed at Fallangia at eight. Mr. Leacock felt the dampness of the river severely, and had distressing pains in his back before morning. On Christmas day he was too unwell to officiate, and it soon appeared that he had been attacked by the dreadful African fever. On the following day Duport was seized in the same way. Mr. Wilkinson attended them with the utmost assiduity, and proved himself an excellent nurse as well as a kind friend.

While attending upon them, the swarthy chief found time to write the following letter to the Bishop of Barbados, who was still in England :—

"Rio Pongas, Fallangia,
Dec. 29th, 1855.

"My Lord Bishop,
"I beg to return you many thanks for having sent the Rev. Mr. Leacock out here amongst us, for the purpose of civilizing my country, in carrying on a religious work, and educating our children, and such as are willing to come to the true light of Christian knowledge; and I am always willing to render the said Mr. Leacock all the assistance that lies in my

power, and to grant him, or the Society, a land to build a church, &c.

"And in the interim, my lord, I have to inform you that I am a native of this country, and now one of the chiefs; but have been educated in England, for which I am greatly indebted to the British nation, and am always happy to render that nation all the assistance I can for the civilization of Africa, my country.

"I have the honour to remain, my lord, and may God bless the efforts you have undertaken.

"I am yours faithfully,
"RICHARD WILKINSON."

Meantime the Governor of Sierra Leone became anxious about the two missionaries. A few days after Mr. Leacock had decided on remaining at Tintima, Colonel Hill was informed by a gentleman acquainted with that place that its inhabitants were the most bigoted of Mohammedans, and extensive slave-dealers, and that, no doubt, they would regard the missionaries as spies of the British Government, and would certainly poison them, if fever did not previously cut them off. He was, moreover, assured that there was not a spot on the banks of the Rio Pongas more marshy and unhealthy, and more infested with gnats and mosquitoes, than the village of Tintima and the country immediately surrounding it. Alarmed by this intelligence, the governor requested Lieutenant Grubbe, of H.M.S. "Teazer," to proceed forthwith to the Rio Pongas, and ascertain the state of Mr. Leacock's health, in order that, if not satisfied with the place, he might be brought back immediately to Freetown.

On the 29th of December, an officer arrived at Fallangia with a kind letter from the commander of the "Teazer," which was then lying at anchor off the mouth of the river. Mr. Leacock and Duport at once embraced the opportunity of returning to Freetown, where Dr. Bradshaw's medical advice would be of the highest importance to them. Mr. Leacock could scarcely walk, and Duport was hardly able to rise, but his companion assisted him to stir himself, and they were both placed on mattresses the next day, and taken on board the boat. In less than eight hours, the tide favouring them, they reached the "Teazer," much refreshed by the sea-breeze, and immediately sailed for Sierra Leone, where they arrived at a late hour on the 31st, thus terminating an eventful year of Mr. Leacock's life.

On the 2nd of January, 1856, Mr. Leacock wrote to me from Freetown as follows :—

" My dear Caswall,
" Although I am hardly able to write much, from the exhaustion which I feel, yet I must tell you I am greatly obliged by your kind letter of Nov. 19. I returned yesterday from the Rio Pongas ; and I believe God saved my life by putting it into the governor's mind to instruct the officer on the station to send up the river and inquire how I was. I was in bed sick ; and immediately, on being advised, I made an effort to go on board, and quit for a time the dead-

ly influence of the malaria. I was soon revived by the ocean's sweet air, and in forty-eight hours found myself in Sierra Leone. Here I found a package of letters and papers, which had been awaiting an opportunity to be sent to me since the 14th of December. And I shall be obliged to *leave* this for you, as I shall embark to-morrow morning for Rio Pongas. I am twenty miles up that river, 140 miles from Sierra Leone, north of it, and out of the reach of any means of rapid communication. Only one man trades regularly with that place in which I live, and his boat comes to Sierra Leone for merchandise once in eight weeks. Other boats are trading with other places, but they will not take letters for me, fearing that they may develop the secrets of slave-trading. The various officers on the coast tell me that this is the greatest slave country on the whole coast of Africa, and if the curse be ever driven from it, it will linger about Rio Pongas as long as it can. * * *

"I am recovering from my attack of fever. I am very weak and nervous; my head swims, and is full of noise to-day, but not so greatly confused as yesterday. I feel as if I had received a tremendous blow on my poor head, from which I am gradually recovering. * * * At the commencement of my sickness, John was very attentive; but two days afterwards he was taken ill, and there we were, neither could assist the other. But God would not leave us to ourselves. He provided a kind old man to nurse us both, and when he had done all that he could, He sent Her

RETURN TO FALLANGIA.   165

Majesty's ship, the 'Teazer,' to bring us to Sierra Leone. So He takes care of his children.

"I thank you, dear Caswall, and your friend Mr Dickinson for the kind resolution you have made to watch my proceedings, and to help me if you can. You shall have a faithful statement of them; and I know, while God gives me grace to seek His honour, and His alone, that He will not turn the hearts of His people from me. * * *

"I want about 50*l.* more than my Society can give me towards my house and church-building. If the West Indian Church Association send me teachers, it will require of them 500*l.*, but I can provide my own after a while at a cost of about 210*l.* I can find occupation for at least *six* teachers."

Mr. Leacock allowed himself very little time to recruit his health, and when the "Teazer" sailed from Freetown on the 4th of January, for her station near the rivers Pongas and Nunez, he and his assistant returned in her. He was able to read the full service and to preach on board the vessel on Sunday, the 6th, and at five o'clock on Tuesday morning the ship was lying at anchor about six miles off the mouth of the Pongas or Fattalah. At that early hour Mr. Leacock and Duport embarked in a small boat in order to ascend the stream to Fallangia. The tide was against them the greater part of the way, and the day extremely hot. They did not arrive at Mr. Wilkinson's residence until about six o'clock in the evening, after a fatiguing row of thirteen hours. After this, Duport

166 JOHN DUPORT BEGINS TO TEACH.

was for some time very unwell, with symptoms of fever; but Mr. Leacock reported himself "quite well," only feeling weak in the knees and ankles. Though he had a good appetite, he could not obtain the diet suitable to a convalescent. Ground-nut soup and boiled cassava were his ordinary articles of food, but he felt perfectly satisfied, hoping in the course of the year to have his garden, poultry-yard, and easy access to Sierra Leone, where many things necessary for his accommodation could be obtained.

On Sunday the 13th of January, he preached in the morning from Philippians ii. 9. 11 (some Mohammedans being present), but was unable to take the duty in the afternoon. Accordingly, at his request, Duport (being now much better) delivered an address to the people, very much to the satisfaction of his superior. On the following day, just two months after their first arrival in Sierra Leone, they opened their school with twenty children. In the evening Mr. Leacock sat down, and wrote me the following letter:—

"Say to Mrs. Caswall I want clothing for my boys and girls very much. Cast-off garments and the coarsest material, so they be light and cool, will be most acceptable. Except in the houses of the chiefs, children of both sexes are naked, with nothing to cover them but the woolly hair on their head, and a narrow strip of blue baft, two inches broad and two yards long, wrapped about their body, *very low* down, in a curious manner, and fastened behind, the end hanging down almost to the ground, and giving them very much the appearance of a monkey. This beastly sight, so thoroughly disgusting at first, has now become so familiar that I can look and not be offended.

"I asked Mr. Wilkinson, ' Is this their own choice?' 'No, no,' he replied, 'they can do no better. Where can they get cloth?' A single garment would be sufficient for each. Any sort of cloth, no matter how coarse, whether it be new cloth or old cast-off clothing, with a bit of tape attached to each to tie before, will be very acceptable. Garments will be given only to the children of the school. It will be better to send what materials you can muster, that the garments may be made here in the school. There is a person here whom I can employ to teach the children to work. This will be a great advantage for them, as they may hereafter be profitably employed in making clothes for the older people. They who are able to purchase cloth, cut a hole in the centre of it, large enough to admit their head, and the ends of the cloth hang in equal lengths about their body, to which it is sometimes fastened by a string or band. Some merely wrap it about their body, tucking in the end for security. The boys seem willing to learn the use of carpenters' tools, and the chiefs the right mode of cultivating the soil. Cotton is the indigenous growth of the country, and I know how to cultivate it; but I want a machine (a gin) to separate the seed. A hand corn-mill, such as is used in the island of Barbados, costing about thirty shillings, would soon turn their attention to the cultivation of Indian corn

"15th. We opened our school yesterday in Fallangia with twenty children. The principal men in the town are sending for their children, who are at a distance with their mothers; and Mr. Wilkinson assures me that in less than six weeks I shall have more than fifty children in the school. He is encouraging his slaves to send their children, but he is the only chief that will as yet do this. He is a strong anti-slavery man. His people are called slaves, but they are in reality free. Several men who can speak a little English have asked to be admitted in the school to take their place with the children. Yesterday evening I had several men come to see me. We sat together a long time, and had much conversation, Mr. W. being our interpreter. One said, 'Sir, you are more successful than most missionaries (he has been much in Sierra Leone); for they have children only in their schools, but men are coming to be taught by you with their children.' May our heavenly Father bless and prosper His own work. I know by this that many prayers are offered for us.

"I have no difficulty here about the instruction of slave children, except it may proceed from their parents, but I fear I shall have to contend with it every where else from the chiefs. I look to God alone for wisdom, discretion, and direction. There are many places on the river in which schools might be established; but at present slave children will not be admitted. I am now waiting for a boat which I expect this week, to proceed to the other branch of the Pongas, called Bangalong, or Big Pongas, and I

SUPPLIES ORDERED IN ENGLAND. 169

shall then be able to ascertain fully how far I shall
be permitted to go with the slaves. Mr. Wilkinson
accompanies me. I have two young men, natives,
whom I wish to put in the school, and train for teaching. Knowing the Soosoo language and some English, they will, I trust, in time make useful auxiliaries.
These will work for ten dollars a month, and be glad
to get it.

"I have never mentioned the box which Mrs. Caswall sent me, nor the kind, affectionate letter with
which Elizabeth favoured me. In truth, till I went
to Sierra Leone early this month, I had much doubt
about the safety of the box. It could not be found
when I left the 'Ethiope' in November; but on her
return to Sierra Leone it was landed in a very shat-
tered condition. The accordion would give out eight
or ten sounds without touching a key. The potatoes
were all rotten, and converted into a most offensive
liquid; but every thing else went safe from being well
packed. The box was too slight. I beg to offer my
best respects to Mr. and Mrs. Blandy, and the other
ladies, with my best thanks for their valuable contributions, hoping that they will not be weary in well-
doing, as they know that in due time they shall reap
if they faint not.

"Now I want maps of Europe, Asia, Africa, and
America, and also a map of the world; some paint-
ings illustrative of sacred history; twenty-four copies
of Robert Sullivan's English Grammar (sold by Long-
man, Brown, Green, and Co., London); four pairs of
scissors; six pieces of unbleached cotton, full yard

170 SUPPLIES ORDERED IN ENGLAND.

wide, or more (pattern sent); six pieces of Indian baft, or, as it is called here, blue baft, which is found in any India warehouse (pattern enclosed); some thread assorted; five hundred needles to suit the cloth; some dozen pieces of broad and narrow tape; some dozen black and white buttons.

"The husband of the woman whom I shall employ to teach the girls to work, has requested me to get for him a flute with four keys. He plays a little, is one that I am desirous to train for a school, and might be useful in getting up a choir. It would have done your heart good to hear the children, after a little teaching, sing one of our chants yesterday.

"Whatever report is issued by the Society for the Propagation of the Gospel respecting our mission, send a copy of it to Ben, and another to Miss A. E. Parker, Perth Amboy, New Jersey, who will be sure to make it known to my friends there, and save me the trouble of writing.

"If the servants and friends of our gracious Saviour follow this example, I know I shall have all I want.

"Believe me yours ever,
"H. J. LEACOCK."

CHAPTER XI.

American Sympathy towards Mr. Leacock. Dr. Coit and the Editor of the "New York Church Journal." The parish at Perth Amboy and the Slaves in Tennessee. Joint Offerings from America and England to Africa. Appointment of an English Secretary. Account of the martyred French Missionaries.

ON receiving the letters quoted in the last chapter, I proceeded to obtain the assistance which Mr. Leacock had requested. He had asked for but little, fifty pounds in money towards erecting his buildings, and various articles absolutely necessary to his mission. I thought it would gratify him if the fifty pounds were to be derived in equal proportions from his friends in America and in England, and accordingly I wrote to our mutual friend Dr. Coit to this effect, on the 14th of February, enclosing extracts from Mr. Leacock's communications. I also wrote, "You perceive that Hamble asks for the trifling sum of 50l., in addition to what the West Indian Missionary Society is able to grant. It has occurred to me that perhaps you and I might raise this between us, as a joint offering to Africa from England and America.

A hundred and twenty-five dollars (25*l.*) from Hamble's old friends in America, including his former congregation at Perth Amboy, would not be much; and I dare say that Mr. Dickinson and myself, with a few others, could readily obtain the remainder, without calling on the Society for the Propagation of the Gospel."

Dr. Coit, on receiving my letter, sent it and its enclosures to the editor of the "New York Church Journal," together with a subscription on his own behalf. The zealous and energetic editor inserted the extracts in his paper, and wrote several spirited leading articles, calling the attention of American Churchmen to the subject, and asking them to assist the "Leacock Fund." The following are specimens of the interest evinced in the undertaking:—

"THE REV. MR. LEACOCK IN AFRICA.—We take the opportunity given by another most interesting and instructive letter from Mr. Leacock, to appeal once more for the small balance yet needed to make up the American quota of the 250 dollars, lately asked for by this devoted servant of the Cross. Read this letter, and see how, at his advanced age, he braves the deadly fevers of the marshy river-bottoms, and bitter and sordid opposition of bigoted Mohammedans and devil-worshipping savages. Consider the information conveyed by him concerning the languages and missionary opportunities of Africa. And above all, consider the door which Providence has so wonderfully opened, in the reception given him by that old native who has been praying God for *twenty*

THE EDITOR OF THE "CHURCH JOURNAL." 173

years to send a preacher of the blessed Gospel to himself and his countrymen."

"THE PONGAS MISSION.—Those of our readers who perused the letter given by us some little time ago, from the Rev. Hamble J. Leacock, missionary on the Pongas (sent and maintained there by the Church in the West Indies), will be pleased to see the continuation given in another column. It is a letter addressed by Mr. Leacock to the Bishop of Barbados, and reaches us, as did the other, by the kindness of the Rev. Mr. Caswall, of Figheldean, England, and through the hands of the Rev. Dr. Coit, of Troy. The ladies will be specially interested in Mr. Leacock's house-keeping troubles—the living on ginger preserves and water, the high price of fowls, the badness of eggs, and the absence of smoothing-irons. But after all these annoyances, we suppose that no Christian can read the latter part of this graphic epistle without emotion. To find that Mr. Wilkinson, an African negro who had been in England in his youth, and there learned something of Christianity, had now been living alone among his heathen countrymen for *twenty years,* longing and praying for a preacher of the blessed Gospel to be sent of God to the Pongas country, is of itself enough to move one almost to melting. But when the old man, greeting the missionary with a cordiality agitated by deep feeling, soon after finds his joy irrepressible, and starting up from his chair pours forth his soul in the glorious 'Te Deum Laudamus,' the glow of heart is contagious, and we are almost ready to sing and weep together with him for joy. Surely, to them that sit in darkness and in the shadow of death, light is sprung up!

"Any contributions made towards the 125 dollars from this country, if sent to us, we shall forward to Mr. Caswall with pleasure."

Mr. Leacock's old congregation at Perth Amboy responded to the call, and came forward to help their much respected friend. From Kentucky and other parts of the West donations were sent, and even the poor slaves in Tennessee sympathized with their brethren on the river Pongas. Mr. Leacock's letters having been read to a congregation of negroes in the State just mentioned, produced an effect which is thus described by their clergyman in a letter to the worthy New York editor:—

"Trinity Church, Sharon, Tipton Co., Tennessee.

"Messrs. Editors,

"At a missionary meeting of my coloured congregation, last Sunday evening, I took the occasion to lay before them the substance of Mr. Leacock's letters, which have lately appeared in the 'Journal.' They were so deeply affected at hearing the condition of their people in Africa, and particularly of those destitute children, that they immediately opened a subscription, which promises to clothe from twenty-five to fifty of them. Please inform me what will be the cost in New York of such garments as Mr. Leacock suggested, made of striped Lowell, and also of transportation to Africa. You will confer a favour also by directing and forwarding the enclosed letter to Mr.' Leacock by the earliest opportunity, and let me know the amount of postage.

"Very respectfully,
"J. A. WHEELOCK."

Mr. Wheelock's letter to Mr. Leacock was as follows :—

"Rev. and dear Brother,

"At a missionary meeting of the coloured congregation (slaves) of my parish on Sunday evening last, I took occasion to lay before them the substance of your letters which have appeared in the 'Church Journal' of New York city.

"At the close of my remarks, the people were so deeply affected by the condition of their brethren in Africa, and particularly of those destitute children, that they immediately opened a subscription to clothe some of them. The proceeds shall be forthcoming as soon as it is closed.

"I wish you to write me any incidents or particulars which would serve to illustrate either the degradation of those people, or the prospect of your being able to do them good. My dear brother, we appreciate your undertaking; you have our liveliest sympathies and most earnest prayers.

"Very respectfully,
"J. A. WHEELOCK."

Not long afterwards I received from New York the sums collected by the editor of the "Church

Journal," which considerably exceeded the amount for which I had asked. In England also, the contributions were equally satisfactory, and I was enabled to write the following letter to the New York editor:

"I am happy to say that I have been enabled to deposit with Mr. Leacock's banker fifty pounds, contributed by English and American Churchmen towards the mission buildings at Fallangia. I have expended the seven dollars from Tennessee in the purchase of three pieces of Indian baft, which were obtained almost at cost price from the manufactory in Manchester. Ten additional pieces were given by friends in this country, together with ninety-eight articles of clothing, made up in Figheldean and other parishes. From the proceeds of the subscriptions in Perth Amboy, and in different parts of England, I was enabled to obtain all the articles for which Mr. Leacock has expressed a wish, such as a corn-mill, a quantity of thread, tape, buttons, needles, scissors, trinkets, maps, pictures of Scripture history, books, and school apparatus. Our good friend, Mr. F. H. Dickinson, requested me to purchase for Mr. Wilkinson, the native chief, a handsomely bound octavo Prayer Book at the depository of the Christian Knowledge Society. Upon this we caused to be stamped in gold letters the name of the worthy old African, and we inserted within, an inscription to the effect that the book was presented to him as the friend of missions in the Pongas country. All the above articles were despatched for Sierre Leone in the ship

APPOINTMENT OF AN ENGLISH SECRETARY. 177

'Ida,' which sailed from London yesterday. Thus the 'Leacock Fund,' in my hands, has taken wings and flown entirely away, soon, I hope, to be replenished."

While his friends in America and England were thus giving evidence of the unity of the Church in sympathy and in design, Mr. Leacock's countrymen in the West Indies were becoming increasingly alive to their duty in regard to their mission. His letters were read in Barbados with deep interest, and produced a feeling of thankfulness that he had been enabled to commence direct efforts so soon, in a place so eligible for the purpose, in the midst of sheer heathenism, and yet within sight, in a manner, of the British flag. The writer of these memoirs, as an old friend of the missionary, was elected an Associate of the West Indian Church Society, and, with the sanction of Bishop Parry, was appointed its Secretary in England. The bishop being about to return to Barbados, the writer was likewise requested to keep up a periodical communication with Mr. Leacock, and to prepare portions of his letters for the press. "Our object," wrote the bishop, "is to have some one more especially to answer for us, and attend to our interests in this country. The interest you have awakened in behalf of our mission in New York, is in every way most acceptable as well as valuable. The embarrassments and trials of West India property, and the many claims on the religious charity of Churchmen in the West Indies, and especially those

8*

of the immigrants (Hindoos, Africans, Chinese, &c.), forbid us to expect much pecuniary assistance out of Barbados, or very much there; so that we are unavoidably thrown in no small measure upon extraneous help, and shall feel much obliged for any from America."

About the same time I wrote to Mr. Leacock to the following effect :—

"The accounts we receive of your proceedings fill us with joy and thankfulness to God. We are deeply sensible of the wonderful providence which prepared Mr. Wilkinson to receive you, and to assist you in your mission. Tell him that the eyes of many Christians are upon him; and that if he continue to persevere, through evil and good report, in sustaining the cause of the Faith, he will hereafter receive a crown of glory. Express also to John Duport the deep interest which is felt in him, both in America and in England, and tell him that many pray that he may become an eminent missionary among the people of his own race.

"The editor of the 'New York Church Journal' has done every thing in his power to make your efforts known. If you will keep me definitely informed of all your wants, I will publish the facts in such a way as shall, with God's blessing, keep alive the growing interest in your cause, both in the Old World and in the New.

"I have been spending a few weeks in Paris, looking into the charitable and ecclesiastical institutions of the great capital of France. I saw much to

FRENCH MISSIONARIES. 179

admire and much which seemed strange and objectionable. The Sisters of Charity are wonderful, and there is a highly interesting establishment of Protestant Deaconesses. At the seminary for foreign Roman Catholic missions, young men are prepared to labour in China, where several of them have died as martyrs within the last few years. Pictures of their sufferings, painted by their Chinese converts, are suspended in the same hall which contains their relics and the instruments of their cruel tortures. Their skulls and other bones are kept in little red boxes with glass windows in front, and are objects of great devotion. Over the picture of a missionary suffering decapitation, I noticed a representation of our Lord holding forth a crown and a palm-branch for the departing spirit. I was shown over the establishment by the student who is next to go to China,—a fine, noble-looking fellow, whom *you* would have admired, Papist as he is. He fully expects to die the same horrible death as his predecessors, and says that he shall willingly encounter it 'for the love of God.' They talk of sending forth a similar mission to Western Africa, where I trust and believe that there are self denying and devoted missionaries of the Church of England who will not suffer by the comparison.

"I am asked whether the Church of England pro duces missionary martyrs. I reply, that she has pro duced many, who, for the love of Christ, have faced death in its most awful forms. It is not indeed our custom, I say, to collect the bones of our deceased missionaries, and to parade them before the eyes of the faithful. We rather prefer to bury them where they die, and, like the body of St. Stephen, to commit 'earth to earth, ashes to ashes, dust to dust,' knowing that the souls of the faithful are in the hand of God.

"Go on, dear friend Leacock, with your glorious undertaking; and may He, who so providentially has prepared the way for you, continue to carry forward your great work until it reaches a blessed consummation."

CHAPTER XII.

The School at Fallangia. Return of Fever. Conversation with Wilkinson. Extent of the Soosoo Language. Need of additional Teachers. Welcome from King Jelloram Fernandez. The Missionaries again taken ill. Continuance of Journal. Duport sent for his health to Sierra Leone. Resemblance of the Negroes of Fallangia to those of Barbados. Conversation with "old Martha." Witchcraft. Second Conversation with "old Martha." Return of Duport. Death of Kennyback Ali. Description of neighboring Chiefs. Agriculture and Animals.

MR. LEACOCK proceeded with great energy with his work at Fallangia, knowing that his life was precarious, and that "whatsoever his hand found to do," he must "do it with all his might." On the 14th of January, two months after his first landing in Africa, he commenced his school, as already mentioned. Twenty children out of the thirty in Fallangia attended his instructions, and, with the aid of Duport, he proceeded to lay a good foundation for Christianity in a substantial education. On the 17th fever returned, and he had to undergo a course of medicine till the 21st, when he found himself relieved. On Sunday, the 20th, he was unable to officiate, and Duport accordingly acted as his substitute. On the 22nd he was able to leave his bed for an hour and a half.

On the 23rd poor Duport was suddenly seized with a chill, which compelled him to take to his bed. Mr. Leacock remained in the school all day, but finding himself unequal to much exertion, desired one of the elder boys to keep the children together and teach them the alphabet, and whatever else he could till Monday, the 28th.

The following is from his journal, addressèd to the Bishop of Barbados :—

"24th. John is better to-day, though he had fever last night.

"Do not be anxious about us, my lord. I state every little circumstance at your desire, and to prepare those who come to us for what they may expect. I think we are passing from the Barbados climate into that of Africa very nicely. As exotics we are doing pretty well. Though we quail and fade a little under this burning sun, we are nevertheless gradually taking root in the soil, and hope presently to be as verdant and flourishing as any of the indigenous plants around us.

"25th [Conversion of St. Paul]. I entered Mr. Wilkinson's piazza this morning, and found the old man reading his Bible *very intently*. As soon as he observed me, he called to me with some appearance of concern, and said, ' Sir, I have been thinking of you.' Some days previously I had been showing him the likenesses of my children, which seemed to delight him, but he could not understand why I should leave *them* to come and live among *naked savages*, but now he thought he had discovered the reason. The

CONVERSATION WITH WILKINSON. 183

place of the Scripture which he read was this: ' He that loveth son or daughter more than me, is not worthy of me. And he that taketh not his cross, and followeth after me, is not worthy of me.'* ' Why, Sir,' said he, ' you must have loved the Saviour more than your children, to come to this wretched place of ours, to look for us poor sinners.' I replied, ' Certainly, father; and I can leave my children in the Saviour's hands, for He loves them more than I do. But read on: there is a promise for *you* here, if you will accept it.' He read the forty-first verse. ' Well,' said I, ' you have received me in the name of a righteous man; your reward shall be that of a righteous man. But read on.' He read the last verse of the chapter. ' Now,' said I, ' if a cup of cold water given to a disciple shall in no wise lose its reward, what will be the reward of him who, besides the cup of water, gives the disciple, in the Saviour's name, a house to dwell in? Certainly to him will be given a house not made with hands, eternal in the heavens.' His expression of countenance manifested a deeper interest as he replied, ' I will do any thing in my power for His sake, and you may rely upon it, Mr. Leacock, I will help you in the fall as far as I can.' Such is his promise. You may live to see whether he will perform it. I have frequent, daily conversations with the old man, and through him with others. We have a little congregation every evening, and very attentive. If the services were performed in a consecrated place of worship, they would

* Matt. x. 37, 38.

184   EXTENT OF THE SOOSOO LANGUAGE.

be called regular public services, with a lecture. At present, they must be regarded as merely acts of family worship.

"26th and 30th. Confined to my room by the sickening intermittent; but when feeling better, coming for an hour into the piazza to get a little fresh air: I know this is injurious, but it is dreadful to be confined to a room, which, for the purpose of reading or writing, is as unavailable at midday as it is at midnight. While seated in a corner of the piazza, examining Arrowsmith's Map of the Western Coast of Africa, the old man came in, and looking at the map, said, 'I wonder that so little is known of our country, for the slave trade has made it notorious enough; and I see countries laid down in which the Soosoo language is spoken as well as in this country.' I may here observe that Mr. Wilkinson has, for many years, been trading with the people of these countries, and that he is still trading with them. Many of them come from a great distance, probably as great as that travelled by the Magi in search of the birth-place of the King of the Jews. Mr. Wilkinson can speak the Soosoo and Mandingo languages as fluently as the English, in which he is not at all deficient in common conversation, or in any subject with which he is acquainted; and he speaks the Fullah language sufficiently to enable him to trade with the people of Futa Jallon (the Fullah being their vernacular tongue).

"I immediately replied, 'What countries?' And to my surprise and delight, he answered, without looking at the map, 'From Cape Verga to the River

Scarcies, and beyond it north-east all the country of
Tálonkadú, Balèga, Sulimána, Timásse, and Tom-
bríchi, the Soosoo is the native language. Go further
south, and in the Timing, North and South Bullom,
and in the Sherbro' countries, the Soosoo language is
spoken. In Sierra Leone too it is spoken, though in
none of these south countries is it the native language.'

"Now this gives us an extent of country, which,
if not as large as the famed Ashantee, is larger than
Dahomey, with this advantage, that missionaries need
learn but one language, the Soosoo, to have access to
them all. Yet strange to say, these great districts of
country to which I have alluded, have hitherto been
entirely overlooked by Christian Societies, the missionary current setting in strong toward the Cape of
Good Hope, and now toward Ashantee and Dahomey.
Why is this ? Is it that the daring chivalrous spirit
of the age overlooks these poor devil-worshippers, and
longs to beard the proud kings, the bloody monsters
of Ashantee and Dahomey ? If danger be sought
for, enough may be found in the climate of the Pongas and back countries, and in the secret machinations
of the poisoner and the incendiary. No open opposition may be expected to a teacher *as a teacher of
religion.* Even some Mohammedans here begin to
say, ' The white man's religion is true ; ' and if asked,
' Why not embrace it ? ' the answer is ready, ' We
have been taught from our youth to believe the Koran, and we cannot change.' The secret is, they dare
not change without incurring the deadly animosity

of their sect. They want that moral courage to meet the persecution that awaits them, which God alone can give. As to those who worship neither Mohammed nor the devil, already three have displayed a great willingness to learn, asking for books, and coming at night to have conversation with us about the common Salvation, desiring to learn to read, that they might read the Bible. All this is encouraging enough, as it shows that a spirit of inquiry is awaking in the minds of some of the people. As soon as I can persuade certain influential proprietors, such as King Jelloram Fernandez, of Bramia; Mrs. Lightburn, of Farrangia, and her son, of a neighbouring town; Mr. Charles Wilkinson, of Domingia; and Mr. Faber, of Sangha, to have their slaves taught to read, numerous small proprietors residing amongst them, and at some distance from the river, will instantly follow the example. Fallangia sets a noble example. Mr. Wilkinson tells his people, 'I will not compel any of you to send your children to school, but you are quite at liberty to do so. I send my own, and shall be glad to see yours come.' Very few, however, have as yet come, for the want of clothes, I believe. They are not ashamed to walk everywhere else quite naked; but when they come to the piazza, and see all the children in the school with some sort of garment on, they cannot be persuaded to enter.

"Here there will be at least five stations, each requiring a teacher. Let him be sent to our Principal at Codrington College. It is not necessary that he should be a person of *rare* scholastic attainments.

NEED OF ADDITIONAL TEACHERS.

Such, valuable as they are in England and the West Indies, and in every improved state of society, would be lost among these people. But he must be 'not a novice, lest being lifted up with pride he fall into the condemnation of the devil.' 'The word of God should dwell in him richly in all wisdom; enabling him to teach and admonish in *psalms*, and *hymns*, and *spiritual songs*, singing with grace *in his heart to the Lord.*' He should know the truth, and know what it is to be made free by it*. The love of God should dwell in his heart, and the ruling principle of his life should enable him to 'endure hardness as a good soldier of Christ,' and to present himself 'a living sacrifice, holy and acceptable unto God.' His life here in an African forest, will have nothing of the ease or comfort of an English drawing-room or parlour; it will be a soldier's tent. Look for such men (no matter whether they be born Episcopalians, Moravians, or Wesleyans), and after sufficient training, they, with our beloved John, himself once a Moravian, will make the number which may soon be required by your missionary. Such is the qualification with which, I respectfully suggest, the teachers should come to us; and when they have proved themselves *faithful men*, and have acquired the language of the people whom they are to teach, let them be admitted into the ministry.

"With respect to the sum necessary for their maintenance, I cannot yet decide. If they be greedy

---

* John viii. 31, 32, 36.

of 'filthy lucre,' they will not answer here, nor anywhere else. In this place it will not take much to support a man, if he will attend to his garden. Land costs nothing. It is readily given to any extent that may be required; and a labourer may be obtained at about two dollars fifty cents per month. I have just commenced the cultivation of a garden, and before the end of the year shall be able to ascertain what amount of aid a missionary may derive from it.

"Feb. 1st. To-day I received from Jelloram Fernandez, of Bramia, King of the Pongas, a cordial welcome to his country, with an assurance that it affords him pleasure to hear that at last a missionary has been sent to his people; and, moreover, that he will do what lies in his power to advance the good cause in which we are engaged. He thinks my position in Fallangia a healthy one, and favourable for the establishment of a large school. He intends to send many pupils, and he will assist in getting up such buildings as will be necessary for the accommodation of pupils and teachers. He concludes with a pressing invitation to come and see him. I hope to see him in a fortnight. I have not the control of a boat, but depend entirely on a neighbouring chief, who, with Mr. Wilkinson, promises to accompany me.

"My lord, the opportunity by which this letter goes to Sierra Leone has offered unexpectedly. I would not let it pass, though with difficulty I sit up to write this note. I have had a severe attack of fever, which has confined me to my bed for several days. To-day I am better, and hope to be out in a few days. I don't know how you will hear from me, or I from you, during the rainy months, for no boats can get to Sierra Leone from April to October, nor to Rio Pongas from Sierra Leone."

Mr. Leacock rallied a little after writing the above, and proceeded with the labours of his mission. His convalescence, however, was but brief, as the following extract will show :—

"John Duport was taken sick on Monday, the 4th; I, on Wednesday, the 6th. He was up and out in a few days; and I am now only, with tottering limbs and ghastly countenance, endeavouring to move about. Just as I begin to gather strength, John is attacked. He has been in about an hour. Here he is, poor fellow, by my side, with a galloping pulse, which, however, is checked by aconite. His skin is becoming moist, and I expect perspiration will soon follow. Such are our present trials; but (blessed be God) He gives us power to endure them. They may, I am told, continue three or four months, or longer; and it is of no use to attempt to flee from them. One who comes to the country to remain any time cannot escape: and caution, temperance, moderate exercise, and a strict eye on the enemy, are absolutely necessary, under God's blessing, to save from his deadly grasp." * * *

Mr. Leacock was confined to his little room during seventeen days. On the 27th of February, for the first time since the 6th, he was able to leave his apartment, and return to his school. His account of himself proceeds in the following words :—

"Now for our school. It numbers twenty-four,

190   JOURNAL CONTINUED.

and improves very much. The little creatures are
most of them dwelling in the village. They are up
right early every morning, and in school by eight
o'clock, frequently before, though it does not open till
ten. There they rattle away, not in play, but in right
good earnest with their lessons, under the direction of
a self-constituted teacher—a youth, himself a pupil,
who seems to take great pleasure in teaching the junior
classes. Every thing at present promises well. Even
our own weak, sickly condition is not unfavouraole,
painful and disagreeable as it may be. The old man,
Mr. Wilkinson, who is an experienced nurse, says it
is better to meet and undergo the evil effects of climate at once, than be attacked by them months hence.
' The sooner the better,' is his saying.*

"Sierra Leone is the nearest point of stopping to
the Rio Pongas for the African steamer, and an opportunity from one place to the other occurs very
rarely, even in the best season of the year. Small
open boats are the only means I have of sending letters to Sierra Leone to meet the steamer, and to take
up whatever letters my agent has received for me.
From May to October the communication by boat is
cut off altogether. The south winds then set strongly
in on all this coast, and make a tremendous sea ; and
the tornadoes, particularly in May and October, are
very dangerous. No small craft can live ; and as to
our little boats, it would be madness to attempt cross-
ing the bar, and putting out to sea in one of them. I

* This is not the most tempestuous, but the most unhealthy season
of the year. The healthy is the rainy season.

mention this, to set your mind at ease, should you not hear from me at the appointed time; and bear this in mind, I have no knowledge of the matter—I hear it from traders and boatmen.

"March 2nd. John much better to-day. Had a full congregation. Though weak, I ventured out, and read a selection of the prayers, and preached. The people very attentive. You would be greatly pleased to see the old man, Mr. Wilkinson, after the service is over, sit down, while the people are yet in the room, and explain to them, in their own language, the subject of the sermon.

"March 11th. Your letter of December 21st I had the pleasure of receiving on Sunday, the 9th instant, after first service. It found me in bed, where I had been confined since Monday, the 3rd, for my imprudence in preaching on the preceding day. I am now very feeble; hardly able to get out of my room. Yesterday I tried, and failed ; to-day I have succeeded, by which you will perceive how much I have improved in twenty-four hours. Your letter has greatly strengthened me; it is quite a lift by the way. I hope I shall be spared the rest of the sickness, and be enabled to *do* as well as to *suffer* the Divine will."

Supposing that Duport's health would be benefited by a little change, Mr. Leacock sent him to Sierra Leone at the beginning of his Easter vacation, viz. on the 18th of March. He commissioned him to select some good materials for the doors and windows of their future residence. He was anxious that the carpenter's work should be done during the rainy season, and so be in readiness when wanted in the next dry season. He knew that it would be lost labour to attempt building mud walls in the rainy season; for what was put up one day would be levelled the next. Duport was the only carpenter he could obtain without sending to Sierra Leone at a considerable charge for passage, board, lodging, and wages. While left alone at Fallangia his account of himself proceeded in the following words:—

"March 31st. I went out a little after sunrise this morning (the first time for many weeks) to see the lot which is appropriated for my garden, and I instructed the people how to lay it out and prepare it for corn, potatoes, yams, beans, &c.: valuable 'flowers' here to me, because not found in any part of the country. They quickly understood me, though I cannot speak a dozen words of their language; and I left them at work, and returned not a bit the worse for my walk and exertions. The fever left me some days ago, and according to my old friend, *not to return again*. I am, of course, weak, and a little exercise shakes my knees.

"As soon as I had an opportunity I called Mr. Wilkinson, and read your letter to him. He heard me very quietly through, and then said, in substance, 'The Bishop desires to know whether I and the other chiefs will render any assistance towards the erection of the buildings. I cannot answer for all the other chiefs, but I can answer for *myself* and my son *Charles*. I, a poor old sinner, prayed God to send us a missionary to show us the way of salvation. He

WILKINSON'S INTENTIONS. 193

has heard my prayer, and sent a man; and now shall
I turn him out of doors? The work is intended for
God's glory, and He will help us; I am very confident
we shall be able to do all I have promised, which is
to build the walls, and roof them.'

"'Mr. Wilkinson,' said I, 'the Bishop may think
that I have fabricated all this, to cause an impression
at home favourable to myself. He does not know the
state of things here. He supposes, and all my friends
suppose, that there are no educated persons in the
country. It is true the number is very, very small;
but they do not understand this. They think you are
all savages. In order, then, to certify them that I
have stated nothing but truth, will you endorse what
you have now spoken?' He laughed, and said, 'Certainly; you write it down, and I will put my name on
it.' So, my lord, here is the promise; you have it as
I received it: and *you* have as much security for the
performance of it as *I.* It is the word of an African,
and we shall see whether the hope which it inspires
'maketh ashamed' or not. I have mentioned all, from
my first conversation with the Governor on the subject of our mission, in order to encourage you to persevere in the good work. Many discouragements we
have to encounter. The zeal of the chief of Fallangia
may help to counteract them; but if it fail, and our
hope perish, your mortification will never exceed mine.
Moreover, by stating these circumstances, it will con-
vince you that I have been led, almost dragged, into
paths I knew not; certainly against my will did I
come to this place. I had instructions, and in obeying

9

194   APPLICATIONS FOR BAPTISM.

the instructions, I have been turned out of the path which had been marked out for me, and brought to a place of which I had never heard any thing. My lord, continue your prayers and exertions for the prosperity of the work, and it will not fail, though the execution of it be committed to the hands of your weak and unworthy servant."

In a letter to me, dated March 14th, Mr. Leacock writes :—

" I had almost forgotten one of the most important points, not being willing to speak confidently of a matter in which one may be easily deceived; I mean the spiritual effect of our labours. We have several applications for baptism, and several serious inquirers. A venerable-looking old man came to me to-day, while writing this letter, and said, he had come to ask me some questions about God and a future state, but he could not be persuaded to commence the conversation, as he saw me engaged. He said he would come again. We have services in our piazza every sabbath, and generally they are well attended. No opposition to be seen any where in this place,—so much for old Wilkinson's example.

" I know not why the stream of popular favour should run down so rapidly towards the Equator and the Cape of Good Hope. There is good hope, however, in the Pongas country. The place is very little known, except to slavers, to whom it has hitherto afforded a rich harvest. It seems to me that it is the very place to which a mission from Barbados should be sent. There is a striking resemblance between the natives here and the Africans in Barbados, or what I remember of them at the time of their importation, and subsequently to the termination of slavery; and even now their amusements, musical instruments, &c., are not without analogy. I have no doubt that a great number of the people imported into our island came from this place. There is a ruined, once a flour-ishing village, on the Bangalong river, called Liver-pool, and there is an impression on my mind that Liverpool took the lead in supplying Barbados with slaves. The musical instrument used to this day by the negroes in Barbados, called the 'pump,' is also used here. The singing of the people here is like the singing of the poor Africans, as I remember it in my youth; the baskets are made here just as they are now made in Barbados. These circumstances, and others, make it appear to me singular that Providence should close every door on the coast against me, except this. This has been opened to me; and I am cordially wel-comed by every chief I have met. Mohammedans are kind, and say, 'De white man's religion is true.' Many are inquiring for the way, and some are begging for baptism; I am holding them in abeyance, till we get up our church. It may be that their desires are of an ephemeral character, perhaps without any solid foundation, and that might be injurious to us just in the commencement of our labours."

Under the date of April 9, he writes :—

" Many parents at a distance from Fallangia are now ready to send their children to us, and nothing but the want of lodging prevents our receiving them.

We intend soon to fit up our schoolroom so as to afford ample accommodation, where they will be immediately under the eye of the teacher night and day. Mr. Wilkinson will board them.

"We had last Sunday and the preceding one but a slender congregation. Polygamists, without any direct allusion to their mode of life, see and feel that it is contrary to the spirit of the Gospel, and Mohammedans (such as have attended our ministry) are equally convinced of the truth of the Bible and falsehood of the Koran. The heathen, too, are not without conviction of their danger."

An interesting conversation is mentioned between old Martha, while sick, and Mr. Wilkinson, respecting the missionary. The former said to the chief, "Now you have got the *book man*. God has sent him to you. You must hear what he says: if you don't it will go hard with you *to-morrow*." On being asked what she meant by *to-morrow*, the answer was, "The next world."

The people treated Mr. Leacock with much respect and said, "This white man does not come to trade with us: he brings the good book to teach us." "But," he remarks, "notwithstanding this persuasion, very few come for instruction. I have had frequent conversations with those who speak a little English, and they have listened, at times, with intense interest. Others, who do not understand our language, after two or three attempts to keep up a conversation have been discouraged. This points out to us that native teachers are to be preferred. Notwithstanding, I trust the leaven is at work. If some understand, others will learn from them. My hope, under God's blessing, is chiefly in the children. The parents may learn something from them, and talk of it to others; and so a few may, after a long time, come to the knowledge of the truth."

"I will now state a circumstance which sometimes occurs in this country, and which proves to my mind that, ignorant and heathenish as the people generally are, there are some who are not wholly destitute of human feeling.

"In most of the villages witchcraft exists, more or less; but it is far from being encouraged generally by the chiefs, as it is reported of chiefs in other African countries. Here it is held by many in the greatest abhorrence. In some villages it is enough that suspicion only rests on an individual, to cause him severe punishment; but when the circumstance is proved, the poor wretch, having a weight tied to him, is thrown into the river, to be devoured by alligators, or he is tied to a stake and burnt. This, however, is a rather rare occurrence. The masters of those slaves who are convicted of the wicked craft, prefer sending them away into the interior, or selling them to slavers, hoping that by better management they may be cured of their wickedness, or by better government restrained from the practice of it.

"Does not this look humane?"

"April 18th.—Several Mohammedans (strangers) came into our school to-day, and seemed pleased with the order and diligence of the children. Having heard the classes recite their lessons to me, one of them remarked, 'The white man has now come to our country, and my master taught me in my youth that when he comes, fourteen years afterwards *the leopard shall lie down with the kid.*'"

"Mr. Wilkinson said, 'I believe that happy period of the Church is not far distant: but no one can tell the day or the hour in which it shall come. It is a secret, and it will remain a secret, till the sign of the Son of Man is seen in the heavens.' Conversations on the Scriptures almost daily occur between him and strangers, or his own people, in their own language, and I am sometimes called to help him out of a difficulty.

"A few evenings ago, Mr. Wilkinson and. I were sitting together in my lodging, when old Martha came in. I invited her to be seated, and soon after the following conversation took place, Mr. Wilkinson being our interpreter.

"'Martha, you and I are advanced in years, and must expect soon to leave this world, what is your hope for the next? Do you know to what place you are going?' 'No, I know not the place to which I am going; but my trust is in God. I never trusted in any thing else, never in any greegree, nor in any god, but the *great God,* from my youth. My father and mother died when I was a child, and from that time I have trusted in God.'

"'What makes you trust in the great God?' 'He has been good to me in feeding and in taking care of me when I knew it not, and could not take care of myself. He raised up friends for me.'

CONVERSATION WITH MARTHA. 199

" 'But, Martha, this He does for the wicked and ungodly. In Him they all live and move and have their being *temporally*. He feeds and clothes them, though they know it not. I admit that God is unspeakably good; but is He not also just? He punished angels, once bright and glorious, who sinned against Him; and if He act unjustly by saving us who have sinned as well as they, how can He be called good? Have you always done what He commands? Have you never left undone what he requires you to do?' 'I don't know what He commands. I never heard that He had given any commands; but I have always endeavoured to do what I thought was right.'

" ' Well now,' I said, ' here is one of his commands (1st Commandment), and here is another (4th Commandment), and here another (10th Commandment), each explained. Have you never broken these commandments? (No answer.) All these commandments proceed from His goodness, and if you have broken them, how can you trust in Him? Have you not abused His goodness, and been ungrateful for all He has done for you? The transgression of the law is sin; and God hath declared (His truth and justice are involved in the declaration) that death is the wages of sin. How can He deny Himself? Will He violate His truth and justice?' Here poor Martha was at a stand, knew not what to answer and looked sad. I immediately opened the Gospel, and showed her how God could be just, and good, and true, and yet the justifier of poor sinners. When she heard that ' God so loved the world that He gave his only-begotten Son, that whosoever believeth in Him should not perish, but have everlasting life,' that this Son did actually die to bear the punishment of her sins, and wrought out a perfect righteousness for all that believe and trust in Him, I know not what she felt, but she looked inexpressible things. 'Martha, will you accept Jesus Christ as your Wisdom, Righteousness, Sanctification, and Redemption, and trust in Him to bring you to God?' 'O yes; willingly.' 'Then, Martha, if you accept Jesus Christ as your Saviour, you must follow and obey Him in all things as your Teacher. You must think how often you have offended God, and pray Him to change your heart. You must be sorry that you have sinned against so good a God: and put away all your idols, and resolve never to return to them, God helping you. You must receive as truth what He has caused to be written for our instruction. Thus walking with Him as your only 'Way' to God, and as the only Teacher of 'Truth,' He will give you 'life,' spiritual and eternal life. This, Martha, is the only true ground of hope and trust in God. Are you willing to take Jesus Christ as your only Saviour?' 'O yes, very willing.' 'Then remember His command to the disciples, 'Go, preach the Gospel to every creature: He that believeth and is baptized shall be saved.' You say you believe, are you willing to be baptized?' 'O yes, I am willing.'"

"22nd. Duport has at length arrived, strong and healthy. I am truly glad to see him, as I do not feel myself equal to the labours of the school in my present weak state, and but for his timely presence, I should be compelled to leave the school to work itself. He is looking well, though he had a week's severe attack of fever in Sierra Leone. He left the day after the steamer's arrival, and, to my great joy, brought your two right welcome letters, accompanied by fourteen others, partly from England, partly from the West Indies, and partly from the United States. I received also the 'Mission Field' for March, and a large basket full of newspapers, which I shall never read.

"I cannot, my lord, express the pleasure I received in knowing that my poor labours had given you such satisfaction; for although I seek not honour from man, but from Him only ' whose I am, and whom I serve,' yet it is truly gratifying to find that my labours are acceptable to His dear servants. Such acceptance *may* be a pledge of His own, for it is He only who giveth us favour with such. Be that, however, as it may, I thank you for your encouraging and friendly epistles; and I thank you further for making the extracts from my letters, which appear in the 'Mission Field.' I thank you, moreover, for the generous spirit you evince in providing suitable lodging-accommodation for your missionaries. Depend upon it, my lord, I will not abuse it; I seek not luxuries; I will do no more than what will contribute to our health and necessities; and I trust, if I live to meet you in committee, to be able to render a fair statement of the expenditure of the means committed to me by yourself and other members of our association.

"Such a house as Dr. Bradshaw of Sierra Leone

recommends*, cannot be built in the Pongas country but at a very great expense. We have a fine slightly elevated site for a house, cool and dry; and mud for walls will serve any of *God's* missionaries, and grass is a cool covering for them. If a missionary want marble and cedar, *we don't want him.* Let him be where he is. I trust, if Satan does not get in and interrupt our work, to erect what buildings we require at less cost than you imagine. Yet I would not have you to be too sanguine, for I am not. I have been too long engaged with the enemy of souls to be 'ignorant of his devices.' I trust in God alone through Christ for help. He has helped me so far; it would be ungrateful not to trust in Him to the end.

"Kennyback Ali is *dead;* Katty going fast,—is already a dead letter. They both deceived me, but I have nothing to say. They are in other hands.

"I expect to leave this week for the Bangalong river. On my return, if I return in time, I shall be able to inform you what use we have for a second teacher. I wish, if possible, to place Duport at Farrangeah. The new teacher I would keep with me till I know him, and till he is acclimated."

Mr. Leacock gives the following interesting sketch of some of his neighbours:—

"Mrs. Lightburn is a native of this country, a black woman, widow of a respectable American white man, who came to this country many years ago, and died here, leaving many sons and daughters, and

* See page 119.

very considerable property. She has a respectable family. Her eldest son, Styles Lightburn, an educated gentleman, resides on the Fattalah river, a branch of the Bangalong. He is a chief.

"Mr. Faber is a coloured gentleman, son of an American by a native woman. He is wealthy, and one of the most influential chiefs in the country.

"I have a new and very interesting chief to introduce,—Stephen, chief of the Bagoes. He is not educated, but he speaks English fluently. In his youth he was put on board of a British ship of war, where he learned true and wholesome discipline; and this training now keeps his people in peace and order. He is a wise and inflexible disciplinarian.

"In all the villages *on the river*, the English language is known by a few persons. It was introduced by slavers and factors or storekeepers, who were Englishmen, or Americans, or natives educated in England or America.

"Agriculture is not much attended to. The sloth and indolence of the natives are unfavourable to the furtherance of any valuable vocation. The chief employment is hunting. Every man has his gun and sword, and is never seen without them. The slaves work a little in their farm-patch, in which they raise rice, coffee, ground-nuts, beneseed, timais or coco, and cassava. This is, as well as I remember, almost the extent of their agricultural pursuits. The cultivation of cotton and sugar is almost out of the question. It requires too much labour for a people who love to lounge in an old hammock all day. They are satisfied with the productions of their farm-patch for food, and a few yards of cotton with which the higher orders cover themselves. The lower class is almost naked. The factors are very successful traders; they spend very little, almost nothing, living chiefly on rice and vegetables; they buy cotton cloth and blue baft, as it is called, and exchange it with strangers from the far interior for hides, gold, ivory, rice, &c.

"I state, on the information of Mr. Wilkinson, that there never was a Christian mission in this part of the Pongas country; but in the Bangalong division, on the Fattalah river, which I have not yet seen, a missionary from the Church Missionary Society was stationed. He remained there a few years, and was finally burnt out. It is now *forty-two* years since that event, and the mission has not been renewed.

"Tell your dear little daughter I pray God to bless her and her efforts for the West Indian Church Association. And I hope the little story of old Martha's willingness to be a Christian will repay her for all her exertions. Say, in answer to her inquiries, there is not a horse in all the Pongas country, not a pig, not a donkey, but here and there a *little* cow, not half the size of your fine English cows. In Fallangia we have many little cows, and I am fed, like a little baby, on their milk, which is very nice. We have cats for rats, and are compelled to keep dogs to sound an alarm when the tiger-cat or the leopard approaches, the attacks of which are very stealthy, and generally in the dark and rainy nights. The

ANIMALS. 205

tiger-cat robs us of our poultry, and the leopard of our sheep; but he has a formidable enemy in the cows. Providence has armed these gentle grateful creatures with very long and sharp-pointed horns; and the moment the leopard approaches they must smell him; at any rate, they all unite and marshal themselves in one solid phalanx, and search for and pursue him till he is quite out of the camp. Woe be to him if they catch him, for they will gore him to death in a few minutes."

CHAPTER XIII.

Assurance of King Katty. Miseries of the People, Visit from Mr. Columbini de Wasky. Application from Cassini. Excursion to the Bangalong River. Domingia. Sangha. Farrangeah. Increase of the Congregation under Duport. Journal continued. Relapse of Mr. Leacock. He visits Sierra Leone, and is ordered to return to England. He determines to remain at his Post.

THE last chapter contained Mr. Leacock's journal down to Tuesday, the 22nd of April, addressed to the Bishop of Barbados. On the following day he commenced a letter to me, which I give almost entire.

"My dear Caswall,

"I received yesterday your letters for January, February, and March. My assistant I had sent to Sierra Leone on the 18th of March to get some lumber, and he returned yesterday, bringing with him letters from November to March, sixteen in number, and a large package of newspapers, all for the last three months.

"Your inquiries respecting Kennyback Ali and Katty, have been answered in some of my letters. The former died a few weeks ago, and the latter

KING KATTY'S ASSURANCE. 207

having come to the funeral and missed me, had the
assurance to write and ask me why I had left Tintima—that I had been consigned to his care, and he
was surprised not to find me in Tintima. I replied
that I was surprised that he should presume to write
to me in that style, when he knew that he had deserted me, and left me in the hand of creatures, who
would have soon destroyed me. I then threatened
him with a visit as soon as I was able to go up the
Bangalong river, when I would tell him how he and
his deceased friend had treated me.

"In my present weak state, I do not feel able to
write to my old friend Dr. Coit. I have too much
writing on hand that I cannot neglect. I am afraid
the application you speak of will be troublesome to
him.

"I don't know whether I ever mentioned to you
any thing about Mr. Wilkinson's baptism. Both he
and his son Lewis have been baptized. It is impossible to say whether the bright prospects before
us are an illusion or not. I am not sanguine in my
expectations. I have only told you of the favourable reception I have met with from certain chiefs,
and of the prospect they have held out to us. You
have it just as I received it, and you have as much
security for the performance of their promises as I
have.

"Your last inquiry respects Jelloram Fernandez
(King of the Pongas). I have not seen him. I am
now hardly able to encounter the sun and rain in
going up the river. We have here neither stage-coach

208   MISERIES OF THE PEOPLE.

nor railway, and a little open boat amidst sandbars
and tornadoes, is a shadowy sort of thing.

"28th. How greatly am I moved with compassion
for the miseries of the people around me. I had
heard from Duport of a Mr. Columbini de Wasky,
who fell in with him on his return from Sierra Leone,
and made many inquiries of him respecting our school
and mission. He had heard in his own settlement,
Cassini, of our mission; and his father-in-law, and all
the neighbouring chiefs deputed him to come to me,
and to say that they were greatly in want of religious instruction for themselves and their children.
Cassini is near the river Componee, which is between
the Rio Nunez and the Rio Grande. The people are
very poor. They have no money, but they can supply a missionary with fish, rice, and plantains. They
will also help to get up a dwelling-house and school-
house for him, and do all in their power to make him
comfortable. The man seemed to be in good earnest.
He bewailed the wretched condition of the young
people in this country, all growing up in ignorance
and sin, and asked if I could do any thing to help
them. He would send over twenty to us immediately; but we have no accommodation for them. We
shall not be ready before January, 1857. He asked
then if we could send them a teacher. He would
prefer a married man, as the people wished their
daughters to be educated as well as their sons.
Here, again, I was unable to give him a satisfactory
answer. It was Sunday morning. He came with a
Roman Catholic as a guide. I invited them at the

COLUMBINI DE WASKY. 209

hour of prayer (they spoke English a little) to go with us to the Piazza, where we meet for worship. The Roman Catholic declined the invitation, but the other was all attention. After service, he came up to me, offered me his hand. and thanked me heartily. I preached from Matt. xx. 6, 7. The room was crowded, and solemn attention pervaded it. The man told me, ' Sir, I have come from Cassini in an open boat, and had to encounter many tornadoes to seek the word of God for my people.' Cassini is said to be 160 miles from Fallangia. But what renders his case doubly interesting is that *he is a Greek*. I could not help thinking that he was sincere in regard to the great object who alone is worthy of our search ; that Friend, who, above all others, is worthy of being known. If our Lord declared that He was glorified by the first-fruits among the Gentiles, may we not hope that the application of one Greek for the word of God, and the ordinances of His house, in behalf of a great district of country, will bring additional glory to Him ? Oh, then, my dear Caswall, apply to your *Society for the Propagation of the Gospel* for help ; apply to the friends of Christ for help. Let them send us a good, holy, pious man and his wife, who knows, and is competent to teach the truth as it is in Jesus ; who is able to teach sacred music (nothing but psalms and hymns), and who by their example may so adorn the doctrine of God in all things, that others seeing their good works may glorify our heavenly Father.

" The boat is waiting for me, and I am summoned to prepare for travelling."

210   EXCURSION TO THE BANGALONG.

Mr. Leacock was now on the point of setting out on his long-promised excursion to the Bangalong River or Big Pongas. Mr. Wilkinson had dissuaded him hitherto from the attempt, under the impression that he was not strong enough, nor sufficiently prepared to encounter the sun and damp dews. Now, however, he thought there was no danger, and Duport having returned to take charge of the school and the Sunday services, he himself volunteered to accompany the good missionary, and to visit with him the various chiefs on the river. His son Charles, the chief of Domingia, offered the use of his six-oared boat, a very comfortable little vessel, with an awning and a place for Mr. Leacock's mackintosh bed. All this was very encouraging, and as yet there was no shrinking from promises or engagements. Mr. Wilkinson, indeed, appeared to long for the time when he might commence his work, and not only his son, but Gomez, the chief of Backia, was pledged to assist and support him.

On Monday the 28th of April, Mr. Leacock and his friendly chief left Fallangia in the boat, and were rowed down the beautiful Little Pongas to Mangrove Island, where the streams unite. Hence they ascended the Fattalah to Domingia, where they arrived at ten o'clock at night. Not being able to land, they slept on board of an American schooner which lay off the town, and next day (Charles Wilkinson not being at home) they again took boat when the tide served, and in a few hours landed at Sangha, which stands on a creek running into the Bangalong. Here they were received very cordially by Mr. Faber, the semi-American already mentioned, who entertained them with great hospitality. Mr. Leacock was compelled to remain quiet the rest of the day and the whole of the following, in consequence of weakness and a slight attack of fever, but on the following day, which was Holy Thursday, May 1st, being greatly refreshed, he was enabled to proceed with Mr. Wilkinson on his journey. They ascended to the source of the Bangalong, where they landed at Farrangeah, the residence of Mrs. Lightburn, the African widow described in a former chapter. They found the old lady a plain, humble-looking person, notwithstanding her great wealth. She and her children owned more than a thousand slaves, and a great tract of country, partly cultivated by her people. They cultivated rice, ground-nuts, Indian corn, fundangia (a very small sort of rice), and Guinea corn, which they exchanged for European merchandise.

After being welcomed and feasted by Mrs. Lightburn, they left her on Saturday, May 3, and returned to Mr. Faber's at Sangha about nine in the evening. On the following day they rested and engaged in the Church services, at which six persons assisted. On the 6th they reached home safe and sound, Mr. Leacock feeling himself much stronger and better for his excursion. He then wrote the following report of the results of his investigations:—

"Wherever I have been, our mission is readily received. Mrs. Lightburn consented to my visiting her place for the purpose of preaching, and Mr. Faber told me that he should be glad to see me whenever I could make it convenient to come. They both made me small presents on leaving their residence, and begged that I would ·accept them as an evidence of their respect, both for me and for the Institution with which I am connected.

"The chiefs are not yet prepared for the religious instruction of their slaves. They think that such a measure would inevitably lead to emancipation, or to rebellion, and, therefore, I have decided to wait till Providence shall open the door by enlightening their minds with respect to the nature and obligations of Christianity and the object of our mission, which is to make masters kind and gentle to their servants, 'giving unto them that which is just and equal,' and 'servants obedient to their masters, in singleness of heart, fearing God.' When they understand our views, I think we shall meet with no more opposition in the country generally than we do in Fallangia.

"I have learned more of the country by my visit to the Bangalong river, than I had any idea of before from the vague information of traders and natives. If it take its name from the river it ought to be called the Fattalah country, for it is properly the Fattalah river, not the Pongas. The Pongas, properly so called, is not navigable more than fifteen miles from its junction with the Fattalah, and beyond this is nothing but a shallow and rocky brook. The Banga-long is not navigable more than six miles; but the Fattalah has its source in the Fullah country, and flows for a distance of more than a hundred and

INCREASE OF THE CONGREGATION. 213

fifty miles. It is navigable for thirty miles from the sea, and would be for sixty or seventy, but for the falls or rapids, of which there are four, and beyond which is considerable depth of water (as I am informed) for some distance. The Bangalong and Pongas rivers then are only branches of the Fattalah--the former commencing at Hurl Gate, and flowing up eight miles (uninfluenced by the tides), at the head of which is Farrangeah—the latter at Mangrove Island, and stretching out some twenty miles, fifteen of which are navigable. I hope I shall not make any serious mistakes, for I am confused by the noise of the school which is held in the next room.

"On my return to Fallangia I was much gratified to hear from Duport that, while *I* had in Sangha only six hearers, *he* had in Fallangia a large congregation on the Sabbath. It seems that during the week he had asked a young man belonging to the school, why the people began to neglect attending public worship; who replied: 'The people cannot understand what is said, and after service are constantly asking me what is said.' Duport then had a conversation with our laundress, who is a daughter-in-law of old Martha, mentioned in my last letter, and a constant attendant at the public service. He asked her if she understood what was preached on the Sabbath. She said, 'No, I do not understand much.' He inquired of her (as I had of the mother) if she was a sinner, or if she knew any thing of sin. She answered, 'No: I have never done any thing wrong.' He then went through the commandments, explaining them, and she said she had never broken any but the *fourth.* The conversation being ended, she thanked him, and said, 'I understand better now.' On the Sabbath, Duport addressed the people, assisted by an interpreter, and he says 'great solemnity prevailed amongst them.' After the service, one of the congregation, an old man, said, 'I like this, I can understand this, and would come to hear it every day. As to Mohammed, I never had anything to do with *him,* and I never will believe him.' The people inquired whether I also would teach them in this way; and upon being assured I would if they desired it, all seemed much pleased. I am greatly encouraged by this, and am glad that Providence has at length pointed out a plan in which we may get a hold of their understanding. I shall adopt it, and use it whenever I can get an interpreter.

"May 9th. Mr. Faber from Sangha visited our school yesterday. He is here to day, and will probably remain till Monday. He is much pleased with the order and improvement of the children, and promises to send two children as soon as he returns home, *one a slave;* and as soon as we have accommodation he will send the four who are now in Sierra Leone at a private school. He now promises to assist in the erection of our buildings. This is an important point, as his word is to be trusted, and he has more wealth and influence than any other chief in the country. I write this from Mr. Wilkinson's information, not from any personal knowledge of my own.

RELAPSE OF MR. LEACOCK. 215

"I have stated circumstances just as they occurred; but if I be disappointed, many will think and say that what I had written had no truth in it, and was only intended to produce an effect at home. But there is One who knows the simplicity of my intentions, and the caution which I have used to avoid every thing like exaggeration or embellishment. I have read my letters both to Duport and Mr. Wilkinson, and they can see nothing to condemn; on the contrary, they declare if I cannot say more, I cannot say less. The letter published (in the 'Mission Field' for March) I have sent to the 'African' press, that it might be inserted there, and have publicity in the very place where the circumstances therein stated have occurred. Surely if I am believed here I shall not be doubted at home."

At the time of writing the above letter, Mr. Leacock thought himself nearly acclimated, and expected his strength to be fully re-established. But the expectation was disappointed. Soon after his return from the Bangalong, distressing symptoms appeared, and he again became unfit for active duty. Fever had left him for some months, but his strength did not return; on the contrary, he felt himself gradually sinking. He proceeded, therefore, to Sierra Leone, in search of medical aid, and arrived at the house of Mr. Pocock, on the 23d of May, in a state of great debility. On the following day, he received a letter from the Bishop of Barbados which cheered his spirits greatly. Dr. Bradshaw came to see him, and ordered him to proceed to England in the steamer, which was to sail in a few hours; but he felt himself unable to endure the voyage in her. She was the "Ethiope," in which he had suffered so much on his outward passage, and which was already crowded with passengers. He begged to be allowed to remain in Sierra Leone and take his chance. Dr. Bradshaw said that his disease was a general relaxation of the system, from which a person so far advanced in years would with difficulty recover. The worthy doctor also signed the following certificate, dated at Sierra Leone, June 7th:—

"I certify that I have been attending the Rev. Mr. Leacock since he returned from the Pongas. He is suffering from extreme debility, consequent on a severe attack of African fever. His constitution seems to be completely broken from his long and severe illness; and I am of opinion that he should not return to the Pongas. And if his recovery is not more permanent and rapid than it has been heretofore, that he should return to England by the first Packet for the preservation of his life.

"ROBERT BRADSHAW,
Colonial Surgeon."

"I am now," wrote Mr. Leacock on the 6th to the Bishop of Barbados, "with kind friends, Mr. and Mrs. Pocock, and I feel stronger already. But here I am, and here I must be for the next four months. It makes me feel sad; but if I were in my sphere of duty, I could do nothing out of Fallangia, in consequence of the winds and rains which prevail at this

A RETURN TO ENGLAND ORDERED. 217

season. I have requested the doctor to give me a
certificate, stating my condition, and his advice based
on it. It may be necessary to satisfy the members
of the committee. I assure you, my lord, I would
not hesitate about returning to Fallangia immediately; but at this early stage of our mission, were my
health to suffer materially, *climate* would be charged
with it, not my age or my imprudence. I see no
more difference in the change of climate from Barbados to the coast of Africa, than from Barbados to any
other of the West Indian islands. In fact, if strangers
will take care of themselves, and avoid the night-
damps and the noon-day heats, there is much less
danger here than in many of our islands. Mr. and
Mrs. Pocock, who were fellow-passengers with me
from England, have never been seriously unwell one
day since they have been here. But their residence
and mine are different. They can get the comforts
as well as the necessaries of life, which are not quite
so easy of access to me. Missionaries in the Pongas
cannot exist comfortably without the command of a
boat. Since I have been here I have been told that
all missionaries, even from the Gallinas (which get
their supplies from Freetown), keep their own boat,
and that we shall not be able to get on comfortably
without one. I speak now only for those who are to
come after me, not for myself; for I must not conceal
the fact, I am not equal to the duty of the mission,
nor indeed to any regular duty any where. The labours of a West Indian curacy I am now entirely unfit for, and I would not take or keep a cure which I

10

218 A RETURN TO ENGLAND ORDERED.

am unable to serve faithfully. I mention this to show you the necessity of sending a suitable person early next year to take charge of the missions. By that time, I trust, we shall have got up a house to receive him. I have come hither with the hope of gathering strength sufficient to attend to the erection of buildings in December and January; and it would injure our mission to keep me at the head of it, when a younger man can supply my place so much better."

The following letter, addressed to me, came by the same post:—

"Sierra Leone, June 10th, 1856.

" My dear Caswall,

" I have not received any letter from the Bishop (of Barbados) by this packet; therefore I conclude he must have left England for Barbados. I therefore send you the letter which I had prepared for him. * *

" I thank you heartily for your letter of May 19th. It makes me feel stronger. The money (collected by the editor of the 'Church Journal') which you will probably receive from our dear friend Dr. Coit, you will forward to me. I will send a receipt for the amount, whatever it may be, and give credit to the Society for it.

" I am in Sierra Leone, under the medical aid of Dr. Bradshaw. He says I am suffering from nothing but debility; but O! this weakness, this shortness of breath, trembling of knees, and cough, are almost as distressing as fever. He positively forbids my returning to my duties till the rainy season has passed by, and wishes me to proceed at once to England. This,

DETERMINATION TO REMAIN IN AFRICA. 219

however, I cannot do, for my absence may cause the zeal of my friends in the Pongas country to cool down, and to postpone the erection of the building in the fall of the year, which would be a greater evil than my death; so I have gained his consent to remain here, and take my chance.

" I knew of your appointment as associate member of the West Indian Church Association. The Bishop informed me of it some months ago, and I rejoiced, and do rejoice at it greatly."

CHAPTER XIV.

Mr. Leacock's Friends desire him to escape from Africa. Letters to that Effect from Mr. Wilkinson, from the Author, and from the Bishop of Barbados. He appears to recover. His Plans for building. Letter to a Young Person.

THE sad intelligence of Mr. Leacock's continued illness found its way, in due time, to his friends in Fallangia, England, America, and the West Indies. All of them, as if by common consent, desired that his escape might be hastened from the malaria which was bringing him down to the grave, and that, if it were possible, his life might be preserved for some years of usefulness in a healthier climate.

The old chief Wilkinson received the information in the latter end of June, and immediately sat down and wrote to Mr. Leacock the following sensible and encouraging epistle :—

" Fallangia, Rio Pongas,
June 26th, 1856.

" My dear Friend, Brother in the Lord,

" I have received your letter respecting the state of your health. I would advise you to go entirely by the doctor's directions: if he advises you to go off for

LETTER FROM WILKINSON. 221

the benefit of your health, do so; but I.should like to
see you before leaving. I have been up to the first
falls of the Fattalah river in company with Mr. William Faber. I almost shed tears when I beheld the
old ruins of the Missionaries' settlement on that river;
but, thank God, I was kindly received, and treated
with all the civilities by the chiefs, more particularly
by Foulah Guyay and Bangua, the two principal
chiefs of that part of the country.

" I am very happy to inform you that our congregation is increasing rapidly. Last Sunday we had
nearly a hundred. Duport is another man since you
left. I believe the finger of God is in this mission. It
is astonishing how the children improve, and how
eager the people are for learning; those who cannot
attend on week-days attend Sunday school. I should
wish you to have a sight of this school before you
leave. I believe, and I am confirmed, that it is the
Lord in his wise Providence who has been pleased to
direct you to open a mission at or in Fællangia. May
God Almighty bless your Society. Wishing you a
speedy recovery, with due respects,

" I remain, Sir,

" Your well-wisher, and respectfully,

(Signed)   " RICHARD WILKINSON."

The intelligence reached England early in July,
and I wrote to my friend in the following words by
the return of the packet:—

LETTER FROM THE AUTHOR.

"My dear friend Leacock,

"Your letter of June 10 from Sierra Leone reached me early in the month, and I forwarded your letter to the Bishop of Barbados by the West India packet of this week, together with Dr. Bradshaw's official cer tificate of the state of your health.

"Earnestly do I hope that you are restored to your usual strength, and that your valuable life may be spared, so that you may place your mission on a satisfactory foundation. But if you continue weak, I must implore you to return at once to England. Here you may recruit, and may possibly be able to return to the Pongas in January to complete your buildings. Besides this, you may awaken a great interest in your mission, and even obtain reinforcements of fellow-la bourers. Could you have an opportunity of telling your tale here, you would see the advantage of being in England *after* having gone over your ground in Africa.

"Should you feel yourself unfit for further work in Africa, you will of course remember what you said about spending the evening of your days with me. Here you would have a bracing climate, and might in various ways, though feeble, promote the great pur poses of your life. Even in this neighbourhood there are people whose spiritual condition is not greatly superior to that of the inhabitants of the Pongas country.

"Since you state that there will be no communi cation with the Pongas before October, and as it is not expedient that the articles should lie longer in a

LETTER FROM THE BISHOP OF BARBADOS. 223

storehouse, I am not in a hurry to send off the things which you desired me to get for you. As the packages will not probably be dispatched before the 20th of September, there will be plenty of time for you to add to the order, or make such variations as you may think expedient.

"I confess, however, that I have great expectations of seeing you here before many days. I think you will, on reflection, feel it to be your duty to comply with Dr. Bradshaw's advice, and I cannot think you will make much real progress towards recovery while you remain in Africa."

The letter to the Bishop of Barbados reached its destination early in August, and elicited the following prompt reply :—

"Barbados, Aug. 9, 1856.

"My dear Mr. Leacock,

"I am not surprised, but very much grieved, at the effect which your trials in the Pongas country have had upon your health. The conclusion to which we must come, you as well as the Board here, seems plainly this, that you have done your part of the work in opening the way, and laying the foundation, which is more than we contemplated when we talked of a mission of inquiry. Even should you think of going back from England (where I hope you now are) in December, which, however, I would rather dissuade you from, I trust it will not be to reside in the Pongas, but merely to visit it, when necessary, from Sierra Leone.

"There will be numbers (myself for one) who will be glad enough to see you back again in Barbados, where I hope you may find yourself again strong and fit for work, and where your information and advice would be of the first importance in conducting the affairs of the mission.

"I humbly trust, and hope, and pray that it may please God to raise up some one to succeed you, and carry on what you have so nobly begun—a younger man, and perhaps of African descent.

"I propose to call a meeting of the Mission Board at an early day, with the view of taking some definite steps in order to make our work and our wants more generally known; and this may lead, by God's blessing, to some offer of service.

"Your interesting letter of the 7th of May, giving the account of the Bangalong river, has been published in the 'Barbadian.'

"The last I have not ventured to publish *yet*. Something of the kind may be done after the meeting of the Board.

"How far is the Bishop of Sierra Leone disposed to ordain Mr. Duport? and how near is the latter to a state of preparedness for ordination?

"I am going now to write to Archdeacon Trew respecting two persons whom he recommends for the mission; but neither of whom would be able to replace you, neither being in orders, even if otherwise competent.

"May God of His mercy in Christ preserve you, and restore you to health, and may He guide and bless us all in our efforts for the furtherance of His Gospel in Western Africa.

" Believe me always

" Very sincerely yours,

"T. Barbados.'

In the mean time Mr. Leacock was regaining a certain degree of health and strength in Sierra Leone. On the 28th of June he wrote to me stating that he was recovering rapidly, and hoped in another month to be quite well. Speaking of his mission, he added, "If we had a school-house, there is no doubt that our report, both as to the number of children and their progress, would be satisfactory; but the advantages of a suitable building we cannot expect before February or March, 1857. There is very little intermission to the rain during this season. When it commences after three or four days' cessation, it comes down at times like a torrent. A few nights ago, such was its force that it seemed as if a water-spout had broken over our house. Now our mud walls and floors, if exposed, could not resist such a torrent. The mud used here in building possesses not, in so great a degree, that property of adhesiveness which is the peculiar character of the clay employed for similar purposes in Wiltshire; therefore we are obliged to build only in the dry season, and to cover the walls immediately with a roof projecting some eight or ten feet beyond them.* Even when the

---

* See the engraving at page 153.

10*

PLANS FOR BUILDING.

walls are cured, were they to be exposed to one or two heavy rains, they would melt to the very foundation. This answers a question in one of the bishop's last letters, 'Why do you not commence building at once?' In September I hope we shall begin to cut timber, and in January to raise the walls. It would be lost labour to begin earlier.

"Our American friends are certainly brave fellows, and our dear Coit among the bravest. Your report of the sum raised by them is cheering. Bless that dear good woman, Mrs. Blandy, for the spectacles for my friend Mr. Wilkinson.

"May our gracious God continue to bless your labours, and abundantly multiply his grace on your dear family, and on all who show mercy to the poor heathens."

About the same time he wrote the following letter to my son, a youth of seventeen :—

"My dear Robert,

"I received your truly interesting and well-written letter on the 24th of May. The preceding day I had reached Freetown in a state of great debility, which when the doctor perceived, he directed me to leave immediately for England; but I did not feel equal to the fatigue of the voyage, and begged him to let me remain here and take my chance till the following steamer. I knew that the timbers in my frame were sound, though they are now old and somewhat *shaky*, and I thought I could trust them. The doctor says that the fever had quite left me before I left the Pongas, and that my present illness arises from debility only, which he should not much regard in a person twenty, or even ten, years younger; but when one has passed the meridian of life, such debility is hard to overcome. I trust, however, under God's blessing, I shall be able to overcome it, and to weather this storm. But I am told it will require great care. I could get no suitable nourishment in the Pongas for a convalescent, and he says, had I remained but a few weeks longer, I could never have left it: my bones would have been laid there. I trust a gracious Providence will spare my life till I am enabled to see to what extent my expectations respecting the buildings for our missionaries may be realized.

"When I shall have accomplished this work, I hope to be succeeded immediately by some person who will be able to do the duties of the mission more effectually than I can. Then I must look for home. My children are unhappy about me, and long to have me with them; and I must say the desires of my soul are after them. I know not, therefore, if my life is spared, whether I shall be able to be in England longer than a few weeks. Most of this time will, of course, be spent with your dear parents, to whom I cannot express my obligations of gratitude for past hospitality; but my increasing infirmities remind me that a quiet and retired home befits me more than any place under heaven.

"Your account of yourself is very interesting, and I trust, under God's blessing, you will continue to improve in wisdom and knowledge—above all, in that

228   LETTER TO A YOUNG PERSON.

wisdom and knowledge which come down from above, and be made a rich blessing to your dear parents and sisters, and to many living and many yet unborn. Do not rely on your own strength. Be diligent in your studies, and at the same time live near to God in prayer, and in the diligent study of His word. You know not how greatly He can and will help you. All his children are taught by Him: it is written, 'They shall all be taught of God;' and unless *He* teach you, you will *never be able* to come to the knowledge of 'the truth as it is in Jesus.' 'Hath not God made foolish the wisdom of this world?' He hath destroyed it: He hath brought it to nought.*

"You know, if a man have not the Spirit of Christ, he will speak 'the words which man's wisdom teacheth,' not those which 'the Holy Ghost teacheth.' And if he make a profession of religion, where can you expect his wisdom will lead him but directly on the quicksands and sunken rocks of apostasy? If the things of God can be discerned *spiritually*, and in no other way, how can any man discern them who has not the Spirit of God? Be not deceived, my dear young friend. Cast all your cares, temporal and spiritual, upon your heavenly Father. He has commanded you to do so, for 'He careth for you.' He alone can bring you to the *experimental* knowledge that Jesus Christ is your wisdom, righteousness, sanctification, and redemption. Depend upon it, this 'cometh not of blood, nor of the will of the flesh, no. of the will of man,' but from God only. *Speculative*

* 1 Cor. i. 19–31.

knowledge is *one* thing, which devils have, and so may wicked men if they will read the Bible; but that knowledge which is *experimental*, changing the heart and principles, and directing the affections and desires in the way which leads to God through Jesus Christ alone, God's Holy Spirit alone can give. Therefore seek it, and never rest till you find it. Then you will know ' what manner of love the Father hath bestowed upon us, that we should be called the children of God.' Then you will know experimentally what you know speculatively, why 'the world knoweth us not.' *

" With affectionate remembrances to your father, mother, and sisters, believe me, my dear Robert,

"Yours sincerely,

" H. J. LEACOCK."

* 1 John iii. 12.

CHAPTER XV.

Satisfactory Progress of the Mission under Duport. Report sent by Duport to Mr. Leacock. Mr. Leacock's Remarks upon it. Favourable Opinion of the Bishop of Sierra Leone respecting it. The Lord's Prayer in Soosoo.

In the mean time the mission in Fallangia continued to make satisfactory progress under Duport, whose youth and African descent were in his favour. He rapidly gained strength, and exerted himself in a manner which appears surprising. He sent to Mr. Leacock the following acccunt of his proceedings, which is too interesting to admit of much abridgment, and which affords a curious insight into the habits and opinions prevalent in an African village. It appears that from the urgency of the case, Mr. Duport, although not yet in orders, felt himself called upon (with Mr. Leacock's approbation, and doubtless with the sanction of the Bishop) to discharge some of the functions of an ordained missionary. It may be well to add in this place that Mr. Duport was ultimately admitted to Holy Orders on the 12th of October.

No. 1.

"Fallangia, June 9th, 1856.

" Rev. and dear Sir,

" I hope and trust that these few lines may meet your health much improved. I am very happy to inform you that I have been tolerably well since you left. Mr. Wilkinson is not here: he left on Saturday, May 31st, for Sangha, and he has not yet returned. Mr. Valentine came to pay you a visit the day after you left.

"I am happy to state for your information that since Sunday, May 25th (Lectures A. M. and P. M., 1 Thess. iv. 13—18), the people have wonderfully increased. At night our parlour was crowded, and we had no room within for those who were standing without. I am now obliged to move the dining-table and my writing-table every night, and yet we cannot make room enough. My bed is occupied, and the mat at the foot of my bedstead is filled with the domestics, who are afraid to show themselves.* Every night we have an increased number. I have made a bench with the board which came from Domingia cut; it is nearly nine feet long. Old Bentra has brought his wives, his sons, and a brother, with three others, to hear for themselves; and they are now regular attendants. This is like Andrew bringing his brother Peter to come and see the promised Messiah. Surely the word is making its way by the blessing of God.

" On Sunday, the 25th, old Bentra told me in

---

* Probably from the want of clothing.

broken English (for he knows a few English words), ' Me love what me now hear, and me pray God open me heart, to believe what me hear, and me country- men.' I told him that if he prayed from his heart, through Christ, God will surely hear his prayers, for He has promised in his word to do so, and he cannot lie; and that though He may delay long, yet He will grant his request in his own due time. After the people left, we had a very strong tornado, which un- roofed the grass on our residence, and the rains poured into the parlour in torrents. I had to awake the boys, and move my bed and table to the only place which was dry and unoccupied; but Mr. Wilkinson had the grass replaced the next morning.

"On Wednesday, the 28th, I had an attack of fever, which lasted two days, during which I was unable to perform the full duties of the school; but the people flocked at night at the usual time for prayer. I ventured to instruct them as well as I was able, but I could not sing.

"On Friday, the 29th, I was invited by Mr. Wilkinson at about eight o'clock A. M. to accompany him and see the Mohammedans make a sacrifice for the free passage of the soul of a woman (who died twelve months ago) into heaven, and its admittance there. I accepted the offer in order to gain informa- tion. When we reached the place, the Mohamme- dans, who, as it appears, were all ready waiting for the chief, arose from their seats, and approaching the cow ready for slaughter, each one laid his hands on the animal, and one of them offered up a short prayer, after which the animal was slain and quartered to be distributed among all the people ; but all who attended our meetings refused to touch or have any thing to do with it. On their sending a portion to John Delone he refused it, adding that he is taught by his ministers not to have any thing to do with such things. They in reply said, 'God bless the missionaries, they tell you true ; it was a blessed day when the missionaries came among you.' This they said because each one, on our people refusing, received a larger portion. It was a day of great festivity with them.

"Sunday, June 1st. To-day the room was well filled ; but since you spoke so strongly against the devil-house and its worshippers and greegrees, * * * has not returned. I have been following up the same discourse, exhibiting the power of Christ by his miracles; and our labour on this point (thank God) has not been in vain. On Sunday night the parlour was over-crowded.

"Tuesday, the 3rd. After evening service some of the men remained behind, and while one of them was telling me how he loves to hear God's word, and no one knows his feelings but God, who alone can see the heart, for man cannot open the heart to see what is going on there, he was interrupted by Thomas coming to me with an open letter in his hand, which was sent by King Jelloram to Mr. Wilkinson, to inform him and his daughter Mammy Sue (our washer) of the death of his son and her brother. The letter came (as I was told) three days ago, and the bearer, being anxious to return, was desirous to disclose the melancholy event to Mammy Sue, but was prevented doing so by Thomas and John Delone, who knew what would be the consequence, and therefore they desired him to wait until they took my advice on the subject. I inquired of them what the consequence would be, and I was told the following. According to the country fashion, as soon as she heard the news, she would give an alarm, and all the women in the town would be gathered together in a moment of time, and would keep a loud and very doleful noise all night and the next day.* They said that the women knew of it already, and were only waiting for the signal. I then sent to call Mammy Sue, and the other women who were on the watch congregated themselves at the door. Mother Martha alone came and took a seat. After asking her about her relations, I asked her how she would like to hear that one of her brothers were called away to go into another country. She said she would like it well, if it be a better country. I was here at a stand, for I could not assure her that he was gone to a better country. After speaking to her in many parables, all which time she was very serious, and had her eyes fixed on me, I disclosed the event to her, and tried to comfort her by referring to many of God's people, Job particularly. I then urged upon all present the necessity of being the children of God, and from that event I

* "And Pharaoh rose up in the night, he, and all his servants, and all the Egyptians; and *there was a great cry* in Egypt; for there was not a house where there was not one dead." Exodus xii. 30.

DUPORT'S REPORT.   235

preached unto them Christ. They listened with profound silence, and, when I had finished, they thanked
me, and each returned to his own home. I did not
forbid her weeping, but I exhorted her to weep in
silence, and pray unto God to give her spiritual
strength to bear this and other afflictions which God
may be pleased to inflict on her, with Christian fortitude.

"On Wednesday, the 4th, we had a very gloomy
morning, and during the day lightnings and thunder-
ings followed each other in rapid succession, and the
rain-waters became congealed before they reached the
earth. It was a beautiful sight to see the people, old
and young, running to and fro to catch the congealed
globules, and sip them, some falling down on their
faces in trying to catch them. Thomas brought some
in a glass to inquire of me what they were.

"Thursday, the 5th. Wherever you turn you
hear the report of guns. It is the Mohammedans'
Christmas. Last month was the month of their fast-
ing, in which they turned the night into day. In the
evening they had a great dance at Lagaba, and our
meeting was deprived of some of its attendants.

"Saturday, the 7th. About five o'clock P. M. I
was sitting in the piazza, reading, and I heard the
reports of muskets, at which I saw most of the people
in the yard running to the gateway. One of Charles
Wilkinson's wives, who went on a visit to her father,
was come. They very soon entered the gate, with
music, singing, and dancing*. Those of our people

* "Now his elder son was in the field; and as he came and drew

236 DUPORT'S REPORT.

who were present, drew back when they saw me.
The procession remained at the gate a long time,
those at the head continually watching me, as if to
say, 'Why do you not go into the house?' I then
turned my back to them, and they very soon passed
to Eliza's house. About seven o'clock Thomas came
to me, and said, 'Sir, you had better keep the meeting soon to-night, because there is to be a great ball
outside in honour of Mr. Charles's newly arrived
wife; and most of those who come here intend to go
to the dance, for they are making preparations, and
they would disturb us.' I told him to send and call
them, as he desired. Never before was there such a
crowd, both within the house and before the door.
Some present had come from the neighbouring villages to attend the dance, and their friends invited
them to come with them to pray first, and then all of
them should attend the dance afterwards. I took for
the subject of the lecture, ' Arise ye, and depart; for
this is not your rest, because it is polluted * ; ' and in
conclusion, referring to the dance, I told them that
those who go and spend the night in frantic mirth,
could not serve God as they ought the next day.
Moreover, that I did not wish to know who went to
the dance, for God knew; I may not see them, but
God saw them. God blessed the latter clause to their
hearts; their plan and scheme were overturned; they

nigh to the house, he heard *music and dancing*. And he called one of
the servants, and asked what these things meant. And he said unto
him, *Thy brother is come.*" Luke xv. 25—27.
   * Micah ii. 10.

left, and each returned to his own home, wondering how I came to know their secret intentions. This was told me on the Sunday morning; and the chief supporters of the dance told Thomas, that they could not make the dance, as I told them that 'although I did not see them, God saw them.' Surely the Lord is in this place, and He hath blessed our feeble efforts with a sign of success. Before they left I invited them to church on Sunday, urging on them the obligation we are under to serve God on the Sabbath.

"Sunday, the 8th. There were present both at morning and evening service sixty-three persons, and at night many more. I again compared the power of Jesus to the power of greegrees (if they have any power at all), taking for my subject the resurrection of Lazarus at the command of Jesus. After evening service old Bentra told me that every thing I said concerning greegrees was very true, for he had proved it himself, and that those that made them were only robbing the people, and deceiving them. Thomas's mother told me that she once had plenty of them, but since we had began to speak about them, she has cast them all away, and besides, she herself has proved them to be all lies; for she had a severe pain in her head, and a greegree was sent her to place on it; she did so, but it appeared to her that the pain increased; she took it from her head and cast it away. Very similar confessions were made by Eliza, Maria, and Mammy Sue. The latter said that there are a great many in the house where she resides, but they are not hers, they belong to Joanna, who is not here.

At night I continued the subject. On Monday morning a woman brought a bottle of greegrees and asked me to destroy it, as she was afraid to do so. I took it from her and have it in my possession. 'Not unto us, O Lord, not unto us, but unto Thy name give glory, for Thy mercy and for Thy truth's sake.'

"But while our prospects are brightening in one way, a cloud is gathering in another. Satan is at work. The Mohammedans begin to be very jealous of us. Some have withdrawn their speech from me. It is truly encouraging to see the young men, who now come to our meeting when they are in the town. Upon these the Mohammedans begin their attack. Yesterday after service they called two of the young men and tried to poison their minds against coming to hear God's word. This they told me through Thomas. They next told the women who have domestic slaves, that we only want to make them free their slaves, and make them as their countrymen in the West Indies. On this subject, by the Divine blessing and guidance, I shall speak this evening, for it is easier to quench the fire when it is first kindled than after it has burnt for some time. John Delone, I believe, is a faithful interpreter; he does not wander away from the subject, but speaks nothing more than what is told him.

"I only wish you were here to witness the change and to build up the little flock, for all want building up and pastoral advice. What can I, a young and inexperienced lad, the most unworthy of God's creatures, unable to build up myself because of my manifold shortcomings, whose only resource is to believe in the precious promises of the Gospel, which all who pray sincerely are sure to receive through Christ Jesus, do among persons just beginning to embrace the Christian religion? But knowing that I am not acting by my own power nor by my own might, I take courage and go on my way rejoicing, because I have a High Priest who can be touched with the feelings of our infirmities at the right hand of the Father, pleading for me and all who come unto God through Him. I beg that you will remember me in your prayers. I pray that God may bless the change to the benefit of your health.

"I must also inform you of the peacefulness of the Sabbath here. The people do not beat the rice nor spread it in the sun. You hear no noise whatever. John Delone has told me that if I had known the town before we came here, I should wonder at the change. This is indeed encouraging. Thomas told me of some of the women who are very desirous to learn the Lord's Prayer, and I am teaching them every night.

"I here remain your humble servant.

"J. H. A. DUPORT."

No. 2.

"Fallangia, June 17, 1856.

"Rev. and dear Sir,

"I have written to you up to Tuesday, the 10th; I shall now give you a few extracts of what occurred since the above date. On Wednesday, the 11th, John Delone brought me twelve greegrees, which he said

240   DUPORT'S REPORT.

belonged to a friend and himself; he further said that
he had paid a great deal to the Mohammedans for his,
and therefore he believed that his could protect him.
I pointed out his error to him as far as I was able, and
he then destroyed his also.   To-day Charles Wilkinson and Gomez visited the school, and the present
chief of Tintima with his attendants. They remained
for about two hours, and then the Tintima folks departed, expressing their regret (as I was told by Charles)
for not keeping us at Tintima when we were there.
The rains have commenced in good earnest; the thun-
derings and lightnings are indeed fearful. I have seen
the people at the report of a loud crash of thunder run
to and fro, so terrified are they. On Sunday we had
very heavy rains during the day.   We had forty-two
persons present, and one of the Mohammedans' missionaries remained during the whole service.   He
comes from the next town, which belongs to that Mohammedan chief with whom you had some conversation not long ago.   He asked to be informed what time
the evening service would commence, for he would be
very glad to attend; but we had such heavy showers
in the evening that I did not see him.   I opened
Sunday school, and we had twenty-two grown persons,
each expressing his desire to learn.   After prayer at
night I was surprised to see old Bentra stop the people as they were retiring, and commence to speak to
them very loudly. After he had concluded, I inquired
of John Delone what he was saying.   He told me that
he said ' the people must return me thanks for what
they had heard, and that they must pray to God for

DUPORT'S REPORT.   241

us; that they must not be enticed by the Mohammedans to stay away from coming to hear what God had
sent to them, and that the Mohammedans are only deceiving them; for the Mohammedans had been among
them now many years, and they never heard any thing
like what they are now taught. He also told them to
pray to God to open their hearts to hear and understand what the missionaries are telling them.' Another
person told me that a neighbouring chief was very angry
the day after you preached about greegrees and the
devil-houses. He said that you meant him, that he knew
who told you that he had greegrees and devil-houses in
his town, and that he did not intend to pull down the
devil-house in his place. Poor man, he deserves to
be pitied; he has never come to service since.

"Old Bentra and John Delone came to school a
part of the day (Monday), and the former told the
children not to speak any more Soosoo; that they
must open their ears and learn English, and many
young people laughed at him, but he does not
mind them; that he is old is true, but he is not a fool,
and they shall not make him one. He then told me
that ere long we shall not find a greegree among the
people. He is a firm supporter of our mission, and a
man of great influence over the people.

" Mr. Wilkinson has not yet returned. King Jelloram has sent for Gomez, I am told, to bring some of his
children to school. I should be very glad if you could
manage to get a bell in Sierra Leone, for the people
told me that when the boys call one half, the other
half know not for a long time, and the first half has

to wait for a long time before the other half comes;
and they asked me to get a bell: also we want plenty
of books for beginners to learn. They have all applied
to me for books, and many have been sent empty
away. If you cannot get any books, I think some
paper printed would do as well; I have tried to print
some, but my time will not permit me to do much of
them. Wherever you turn you hear the people learning the A, B, C; Mammy Sue has surpassed all as yet.
She is in words of three letters. I teach her myself
every night after prayers. All the boys are teachers;
each of them having a certain number of persons to
teach. After school, and at night, I cannot find one
to do any thing for me; they are all scattered among
their relatives and friends. Johnson, Thomas, Richard, and Charles, one of the lower boys, assist me in
the Sunday school. I shall form six classes. The
Sunday school is between the two services. Charles
Wilkinson has told me that he has a plenty of nails,
which he can let you have at 4d. a pound. I told him
I would let you know of it, and he says that his father
ought to commence at once to cut the sticks for the
building during the rains. I asked him to speak to
his father about it, and he has promised to do so. Be
pleased to remember me to Mr. Pocock and family
when you see him. I am quite well at present (thank
God). May the Almighty Disposer of all events enable you soon to return to your momentous charge,
and strengthen you both in body and soul to perform
your arduous duties, is the sincere prayer of your
humble and obedient servant,

"J. H. A. DUPORT."

No. 3.

"Fallangia, June 23, 1856.

" Rev. and dear Sir,

" Mr. Wilkinson returned on the 19th, and brought two boys from Mr. Faber for the school. On Friday night last, Mr. Wilkinson called his people to him, and enforced a law against Sabbath profanation. They assembled in the piazza, seventy persons in number, and after his asking who made them, the world, and all things which they see, and their answering, he addressed them at large; after which we had evening services as usual, and the people went away much gratified with what they had heard. On Saturday we had very heavy rains. Yesterday we had eighty-four persons present in the services, and thirty-five grown persons in the Sunday school. At night we had a large congregation, and in the services profound silence prevailed, and a great earnestness seemed to beam in the countenances of the audience. In the morning I lectured from Isa. i. 16, ' Cease to do evil, learn to do well;' in the evening, from ' All have sinned and come short of the glory of God.' I shall now give you the plan of teaching I have adopted.

" 1st. As I enter the school, the children repeat the morning hymn, then prayer; after prayer they repeat the psalms in the Prayer Book, which they have learned or are learning, then the Ten Commandments and the Creed, with its questions and answers given in the Church Catechism. Then I examine each child from my vocabulary of words, in Soosoo and English. 2nd. Reading and spelling, counting, weights and measures, numeration and the multiplication table up to five times; then arithmetic :—I use mangoes and the fingers to give them some idea of addition. Thomas is in multiplication by four. In reading, every child must give the Soosoo words for the English, and I forbid any child speaking Soosoo in school or in my hearing, on pain of being punished, and it is indeed wonderful to see the change, as Mr. Wilkinson himself expressed to me. Then 3rd. Play hour. 4th. Reading and spelling, writing and dictation; the map of the Holy Land and the many places in it which occur in the New Testament; the distinction between the globe and the map; the distribution of land and water, and the effects produced by the rotation of the earth on its own axis. 5th. Evening hymn and other psalms; then evening prayer.

"I have translated the Lord's prayer into the Soosoo, corrected by Mr. Wilkinson; and I begin to teach it to the children to-day. I open the Sunday school by prayer, and I teach by rote to 'Gloria Patri,' 'Praise God from whom,' &c.; then I teach them the letters, after which I explain and teach them many of the words which occur in the Prayer Book; with the latter they are much delighted. Some of the young men come to school at night, and when they have time, through the day. So anxious are the people to learn, that wherever you turn you hear nothing but A, B, C. Greegrees, I am told, are all nearly abolished. God grant that his word may prosper to the honour and praise of His name.

"The morning and the evening are very dreary

indeed; the Sunday school and evening school I find very laborious work, but my heart and soul are in the work, and it will soon become easy, I hope. On Sunday, for the first time, I saw some of the women and young men begin to aid our voices in joining us. I have removed the table from the church, and have planted a block of wood in the earth, and nailed a piece of board in the form of an inclined plane in the place where you stood to lecture the last Sunday you were here. I was obliged to make some more benches in order to afford accommodation to the people. Old Bentra is very anxious to be baptized. I have sent you the Lord's Prayer in Soosoo, which I trust you may be pleased with. I have begun the creed."

[The following was added by Mr. Leacock.]

"My catechist's report terminates here. Why it should end so abruptly I know not. It may be that he was in school when the boatmen called for the letter, and had not time to proceed with the report. It will now be perceived that my sickness has not been detrimental to the work in Fallangia. For several weeks before I left I had not been able to preach more than once on the Sabbath, and during the week had evening services and conversations occasionally with some of the people. The heathen continued to treat me with uniform respect, but the Mohammedans began to receive my salutations *coldly.* My absence, it seems, was their opportunity to give vent to angry feeling; but I trust Duport will be strengthened to

246 DUPORT'S REPORT.

suffer that, or any thing else, which may come upon him."

Speaking of the chief who was angry with the sermon against *devil-houses*, Mr. Leacock says:—

"*He* was one that promised much, but I told Mr. Wilkinson he would not fulfil his engagements. He loves his idols, and after them he has gone. I am not, however, without hope that the lost sheep may yet be found and brought to the fold. 'Tis true, 'with man this is impossible, but with God all things are possible.' The bearer of this letter to me gives a fearful account of his perils by sea, and says that he would not for any consideration venture to return to Fallangia during the rest of the wet season."

The Bishop of Sierra Leone was much pleased on seeing Duport's report, and wrote to Mr. Leacock the following note :—

"Fourah Bay, July 28, 1856.

"My dear Sir,

"Many, many thanks to you for sending the enclosed. A more interesting and encouraging account I have never seen. May the Lord bless and prosper the work, and make Duport an instrument of extensive usefulness to that interesting people.

"I remain,
"Yours faithfully,
"J. W. Sierra Leone."

THE LORD'S PRAYER IN SOOSOO. 247

THE LORD'S PRAYER IN SOOSOO, TRANSLATED BY MR. DUPORT.

A—AH.

Woung   Fáfa,   Makángua arréyanná,   Ekele Senèyankee
Our   Father,   that is there in heaven,   Thy name hallowed be.

Ekha   yámaná fa.   Esagwánáningáma donu,   anákhèná arreyanná.
Thy   kingdom come. Thy will be done on earth,   as it is   in heaven.

Mookookeetò mŏkŏkee locŏ locŏ tarmera Annoo emookoo younoobee
Give us to-day   our   ́daily   bread,   and   our   trespasses

caffáree mookoofang caffáree mookoolòràbà. No enámo mookoora-
forgive,   as we   forgive our neighbours,   and lead us not

soo   fàkòbee   Emookoorámènè lákóbee: Etanangbà yámanàra
into temptation,   deliver us   from evil; For thine the kingdom,

saimbàra annoo daraja Abada annoo abada. Amena.
the power, and the glory,   for ever and ever.   Amen.

CHAPTER XVI.

Continued improvement in Mr. Leacock's Health. Letter to his Son. Letters to the Bishop of Barbados. Letter to the Author. Mohammedan Opposition. Assistance from Governor Hill. Contest between Christ and Mohammed. Last Letters of Mr. Leacock.

THE report of the proceedings of his assistants in Fallangia relieved Mr. Leacock of a load of care, and encouraged him to hope that even in the event of his own removal, the mission would continue to prosper. But his health was improving, and he loooked forward with delight to his return to the Pongas country, and to a renewal of his truly apostolic labours.

The following was written to his son, already known to the reader as a clergyman at Mobile, in Alabama :—

"Freetown, Sierra Leone, July 12th.

"My dear Ben,

"Although I have written to your sister, and requested her to let you know that I am still alive—that I am not devoured by sharks or savages, nor consumed by burning fever—yet I cannot forbear dropping a line to you to comfort you with the assurance

LETTER TO HIS SON. 249

that God has hitherto heard your prayers for the preservation of my life in the midst of many dangers, and
to beg that you will persevere in the discharge of that
acceptable duty.

"I cannot describe to you what the loneliness of
my situation would be, if my heart were not interested in my work. Except my friend Mr. Wilkinson,
I have no neighbour to associate with when at home.
My residence is a mud house covered with grass. The
floor and walls are all mud, which gives me a sensation of dampness during wet weather, and coolness
during the hot season. As to my bed-room, it is always so dark that in midday it is as useless to me for
purposes of reading or study as in midnight. Even
when I shave in the morning, or at any other time, I
am obliged to resort to the candle or lamp for light;
and then I take my solitary walk, or ponder over the
blessed word. But the sacrifice, as many call it, is
no sacrifice to me, for I am fully satisfied that God
has called me to it. I trust, whatever may happen to
me, I am in the right way, and that is enough.

"I am to remain quietly in Sierra Leone till November. I came hither for the advantage of medical
aid and good nourishing food. From the 24th of
December to the 23d of May intermittent fever had
been trying my constitution, and would finally have
laid me under the sod, if a gracious Providence had
not sent me to this place. I am gathering strength,
but cannot return to the Pongas, the ocean being one
barrier, and the governor, bishop, and doctor's inter-
dict another. So here I am to be till November.

LETTER TO HIS SON.

"I received letters from you both by the June and July packets. Thank you, my dear son, for them. They are quite a cordial to my soul. I pray God to shed a benign and sacred influence over your heart and over all your labours, and make you a rich blessing wherever you go.

"Remember me affectionately to your uncle and his family. Congratulate him on the marriage of his daughter, and I earnestly pray that she may enjoy all the happiness which, in this transitory and wretched life, may be good for her.

"I am, my dear Ben,
"Your faithful and affectionate father."

He enclosed Duport's document to the Bishop of Barbados, together with the following letter :—

"Freetown, Sierra Leone, July 21, 1856.

"My Lord,

"I received on the 12th inst. your letter, dated 'Southampton, June 17th,' the day on which you left England for the West Indies. I had written by the May steamer, and enclosed that letter to Dr. Caswell, supposing that, as I had no letter in May from you, you and all your family had embarked for the West Indies. I have nothing now to communicate respecting the mission from *my own personal knowledge*, being far away from it; nor any thing concerning myself, save and except that my health is greatly improved, and that, if wind and sea permitted, I would return immediately to my duties. The accompany-

LETTER TO THE BISHOP OF BARBADOS. 251

ing report, however [see the previous chapter], will give you a correct view of the general state of the mission. I received it from Duport two days ago. It is not what I wrote to him for. I wished him to give me a statement of the condition and prospects of the school; for I considered it high time that our committee in Barbados, and friends in England, should know *what was actually done.* Having heard that our way was so providentially opened and cleared to commence operations, they would natually *expect,* as well as *desire,* to know what we were about. I wished therefore for a sort of schedule, showing the progress of each class in the school, which would not occupy more than a page of this sheet; instead of which he has sent me a volume of notes from his journal, containing much of what I have long expected, and much that *I* never expected to see, but cherished the hope that it would be the privilege of my successor. The opposition of the Mohammedans I did expect; it has long been working in secret against us, and the opportunity only was wanted to spring the mine. The general outburst of zeal among the heathen for the truth, and the destruction of their greegrees, are effects of our ministry which I never expected to see, so stupid and besotted have the people in general appeared. I believe that, under God, all may be attributed to the convictions of two men, Bentra and John Delone, who have great influence in the village, and who have been long under our instruction. The cause of the Mohammedans' opposition is obvious: 'their craft is in danger of being set at nought.'

Their chief means of support is making and selling to the heathens charms or amulets, which they call 'greegrees.' Each greegree consists of a few words of the Koran, written in Arabic, and enclosed in a leathern case. The warrior rushes into battle covered with these charms, for each of which he has perhaps given four or five dollars; and when, notwithstanding, he receives the deadly wound from the adversary's sabre or unerring bullet, the Mohammedan's cry is, 'His time is come.' The preservation of health and life, down to the hour of death, they ascribe to the power of greegrees; but death, let it come when or how it may, comes *at the appointed time.* When the heathen see no greegrees in our mission-house or attached to our person, and hear us denounce them in most faithful and unequivocal terms, I dare say that some of them come over to us in order to save their money. This may not be a correct judgment, but the people are certainly very penurious, and the excitement appears to me too great to be durable.

"I send you the Report, as I believe it all to be true. There is much in it which I *know* to be true, and which will confirm my former statements. He calls for elementary school-books: I sent for a supply in March, and I expect it in September. He asks for a bell: I have been inquiring months ago for one, and have only now succeeded. I got a tolerably good one from a condemned slave-ship, which has been recently captured; it cost only 2*l.* 2*s.*

"The clamour of the Mohammedans does not trouble me. I am glad of it; for if their influence on the poor superstitious heathen were not yielding,

LETTER TO THE BISHOP OF BARBADOS. 253

we should not hear from them. This is indeed 'a day of small things,' but it is not to be despised.

"I have not been idle since I have been here. I petitioned the governor and council for help, and I have a promise, but I don't know to what amount. My petition was received most graciously. Mr. Wilkinson is still firm, as you may suppose from a letter which I shall enclose with this. As he seems grateful to the West Indian Church Association, it may not be a compliment thrown away if he be nominated and received as *an honorary member of the association.*

"26th.—I have engaged a young man who has been in the employ of the Church Missionary Society to assist Duport in the school. I hope that the grant of the Sierra Leone council will be sufficient for his maintenance. I have agreed to give him 30*s.* a month for the first quarter; and if I approve of him, 2*l.* per month for subsequent services. When he has experience enough to take charge of a school, I shall have to *add* 10*s.* per month; and if the colonial grant be not sufficient to meet the expense, I shall be compelled to draw on the treasurers of the Society for the Propagation of the Gospel. Duport wants help now, and I shall require all his time when engaged in building. I trust it will meet your lordship's consent, and the consent of the committee. Commending the mission to the favourable consideration of all who love the truth, and to their continued supplication and prayer,

"I remain, my Lord,
"Your Lordship's faithful servant,
"H. J. LEACOCK.'

"August 5th.—I have just been informed by a member of council, that the governor has appropriated 40*l. per annum* out of money placed by the council at his disposal, for the use of our mission, subject of course to the approval or otherwise of the Secretary of State. Perhaps a line from your lordship to the Secretary will secure, not only a confirmation, but an extension of the grant, which might easily be effected by withdrawing from false, treacherous, horrid chiefs, the many hundred pounds (I believe over 700*l.*) which are given to suppress the slave-trade, but which only furnish them with capital to go more deeply into it. Educate and civilize the people, and away goes the whole fabric of Mohammedanism, heathenism, and slavery.

"7th.—The governor informed me this morning that he could give me no more than 30*l.* this year, but he hopes to increase it next year. He himself is ready with all his heart to help us, and he says there was not one dissenting voice in the council. The respectable people in Freetown are favourable to our mission, and one gentleman said to me, 'If you have any great difficulty in getting up your buildings we will help you.'"

To myself, Mr. Leacock wrote on the 25th of July. In reference to Duport's statements he said :—

"I do not in the least doubt his statements; for the condition of things was such when I left the country as led me to believe that an outbreak would somehow and somewhere soon take place. The oppor-

CONTEST BETWEEN CHRIST AND MOHAMMED. 255

tunity only was wanted to enable the Mohammedans to throw off the mask. The work is begun, and I know not where it is to end. A diversion in our favour is, however, wrought in or among the heathen, and I trust, if trouble comes, God will give us grace to 'glorify Him in the fires.' For myself I have no fear, and I should be quite satisfied were I alone. But Mr. Wilkinson is a host in himself, and God who has raised the storm will, I know, be at the helm. The only thing which troubles me is, I am not at my post, nor can I get there till November.

"This is entirely a contest between Christ and Mohammed, and we know, whatever the consequences may be, who will finally prevail. With consequences I have nothing to do; but my constant prayer is: 'Thy kingdom come; thy will be done in earth as it is in heaven.'"

The last letter to his dear son in Mobile, bears the date of August 12th.

"My dear Ben,

"An American vessel leaves this port in a few days for Philadelphia, and I cannot let it depart without a few lines to let you know, first, the state of my health, and, secondly, the state of my mission.

"My health is almost restored; I have had no return of fever since I came to this place. My appetite is good, and my strength is greatly increased. The only thing which retards my entire recovery is the constant heavy rains, which prevent my using such exercise as is necessary either for the restoration or preservation of one's health. I have seen rain fall in the West Indies, and during midsummer in the United States, but I never saw any like what falls sometimes in Africa, either as regards duration or heaviness. When it is accompanied by a tornado, it at first comes rushing down as if it would sweep the house into the ocean, just as when accompanied in the West Indies by a hurricane. Then it rains sometimes for a week with scarce any intermission. Tornadoes occur chiefly in May, September and October, but they have not the power of a West Indian hurricane. They up-root trees, and strip off the covering of thatched houses. Seldom do they leave greater traces of their visits.

"Now with regard to my mission. It is well for me that the Lord sent me to this place, for I know not what consequences the present excitement in Fallangia would have had on my emaciated state of health, had I remained in the Pongas country. During all my sickness, except indeed when prostrated by fever, and unable to sit up, I preached every Sabbath, and had an evening service in my room which was generally crowded. The eyes of the heathen soon became opened to the danger of their state, and to the deceptions practised upon them by the Mohammedans. These deluded creatures had been making great gain of them by inducing them to purchase what they call 'greegrees' or amulets, which they made them believe would preserve them from all injuries and sickness, and from every possible evil, even death. The poor

LETTER TO HIS SON. 257

heathen are so stupid, so besotted, as to believe the followers of the false prophet, who are regarded by them as the Scribes and Pharisees of old were by the Jews; and would give for their vanities, four, five, or even six dollars—a heavy sum for these poor creatures.

"These Mohammedan teachers are the principal opponents of the Gospel. At first they admitted that the white man's religion was true; and when asked, 'Why then do you not embrace the truth,' they would reply, 'The Koran suffers us not to change.' Then they endeavoured to reconcile the Bible to the Koran; but finding it impossible, their malice was excited against us. They tried to draw away the young as well as the old from us; but this failing, and perceiving that 'their craft was in danger to be set at nought,' they were full of wrath, and declared open war against the Bible. The heathen in Fallangia have burned their greegrees, are resolved to be carried away no longer by these foolish idols, and are calling for the knowledge of our own God. The Sabbath worship is well attended, also the week-night service, and the Sunday school chiefly by adults. Thus our mission may be said to prosper. The stillness of spiritual death is broken, and although the sword is not yet actually unsheathed, the false peace which prevailed in Fallangia is banished. 'I came not to send peace on earth,' says our Lord, 'but a sword.' I know not how soon this may be drawn: but *I would that I were there.* It is, however, impossible that I can leave this place before November.

258   LETTER TO THE BISHOP OF BARBADOS.

"I am delighted to hear that our American brethren in the western country are 'coming up to the help of the Lord.' We want their prayers as well as their liberality. Both will greatly assist us, and call forth the gratitude of our Association. New York is also coming to our help, as Caswall informs me. The Lord our God bless and help all who help us and pray for us."

The following letter to the Bishop of Barbados, written just before the sailing of the steamer, was probably the last which proceeded from his pen.

"Freetown, August 13, 1856.

"My Lord,

"The steamer leaves at five P.M., and whether it be from the habit of writing to you by every packet during the last nine months or not, I cannot let her now go without a line to your lordship. I have enclosed a letter to you in my heavy despatch to Dr. Caswall, which, in consequence of his having to make extracts for the 'Mission Field,' may not leave Southampton till next month. Duport writes encouragingly, and leaves me to hope that the mission is established; and that too, before a foundation stone is laid for a building. I am not boasting. I have nothing to boast of; for the work has been carried on from the beginning by an agency secret but powerful. 'It is the Lord's doing, and it is marvellous in my eyes.' I trust that many will rise up in that benighted country to call Him blessed. All this is, I believe, in answer to prayer. The Father hath said to the Son,

'Ask of me, and I shall give thee the heathen for thine inheritance, and the uttermost parts of the earth for thy possession.' If the Saviour be reminded of this promise, will he not hear the supplication of His people who ask the salvation of the poor heathen? If faith and prayer were in greater exercise, soon would the wilderness and the solitary place be glad for them, and the desert rejoice and blossom as the rose.'

"In my letter to you which you will receive probably by the packet after the one which brings you this, I have stated that the governor and council have given me a small lift for this year, and encouragement to hope for something better next year. The governor will endorse my draught on the colonial treasury immediately for 30*l.*; and he *hopes* to help me to a greater extent next year, but he is very cautious ; and so precarious and unsettled are things in this colony, that he does not like to bind himself to any sum. I enclose his letters which I received on the occasion. My health is very good.

"Believe me, my Lord,
"Your faithful and obedient servant,
"H. J. LEACOCK."

CHAPTER XVII.

Articles despatched from England for the Mission. Shipwreck of the "Ida." Death of Mr. Leacock. Letter from the Rev. F. Pocock. Letter from Mr. Duport. Lamentations at Fallangia and Sierra Leone. Letter from the Bishop of Sierra Leone. The mournful news reaches America and the West Indies. Eulogy in the "Barbadian." Concluding Letter from Mr. Duport. Funeral Anthem.

THE time of year had arrived at which Mr. Leacock had desired the articles necessary for his mission to be forwarded to Sierra Leone. Accordingly, early in September, I proceeded to London in order to make the purchases ordered by him, little thinking that the intrepid servant of God was already beyond all earthly wants. The following goods were shipped on board the "Ida," a fine screw steamer, on the 15th of September.

A corn-mill, with fly-wheel.

Three pieces of grey Indian baft, purchased with the contributions of the Tennessee slaves.

Nine other pieces of baft.

Parcel containing tape, cotton, buttons, needles, thread, scissors, &c.

Parcel of Scripture prints.

Parcel of light clothing for negroes.

Ninety-eight articles of similar clothing, made up by ladies in Figheldean and the neighbouring parishes.

Box of trinkets for presents.

Box containing maps, school books, prints, cards, and other necessaries for the school, purchased of the Society for Promoting Christian Knowledge.

Box containing school apparatus, purchased at the Depository of the National School Society.

A clock for the school.

A handsome Prayer Book, presented to Mr. Wilkinson by Mr. Dickinson.

The above articles, by Mr. Leacock's directions, were packed in strong wooden cases, not too large or heavy to prevent their being carried to Fallangia in canoes. The insurance and freight having been paid, and the money raised in England and America for the mission buildings having been deposited with a London banker subject to Mr. Leacock's order, I felt satisfied that all had been done which present circumstances seemed to demand.

Soon after returning from London, I was distressed by the intelligence that the "Ida" had been lost at sea in a dreadful gale, which commenced before the ship had cleared the Channel. I went again to London on the 7th of October, with the view of recovering the insurance and re-purchasing the articles, without loss of time. While engaged upon this business, I received the following letter from the Rev. Mr. Pocock of Sierra Leone.

262   DEATH OF MR. LEACOCK.

"Freetown, Sierra Leone, Sept. 18, 1856.

"My dear Mr. Caswall,

"It is my painful task to inform you of the death of your dear friend, Mr. Leacock. When the last mail left for England he appeared in good health, and was hoping, after the rains, to resume his work in the Pongas country. How mysterious are the ways of God! Mr. Leacock came to our house very, very ill, on the 20th of May, but was so far recovered that we all were glad to see him daily gaining his usual health and strength.

"On the 15th of August he was taken ill and complained of his cough, and in a day or two diarrhœa came on, and the poor invalid had not strength to bear such a pull down, and gradually sunk lower and lower. From Sunday to Wednesday he was perfectly insensible, and on the 20th of August, at twenty minutes to six P.M., he truly fell asleep in Jesus. Every thing was done for him that could be done. Doctor Morphew and Dr. Bradshaw came to him often six times a day, and Mrs. Pocock tended him. He often thanked us, and said God had sent dear children to tend and care for him in his last days; and I do assure you, my dear sir, it was indeed a privilege to have had the dear one with us. Had he been in the Pongas country, we should have feared the aged servant of God had not been cared for.

"On Wednesday, August. 13, the dear departed for the last time took evening prayer for me, and spoke to us from Rev ii. 12 to 17. On Thursday he was poorly, but walked out with me, and on Thursday evening went to bed in good spirits, but never again was able to leave his room. Although from Thursday he feared the worst, yet we all fancied and hoped, when the cold was better he would be among us again, and I am sure he would have told me many things had he thought he would so soon be taken. The funeral took place on the 21st. The body was taken to the Cathedral, and the bishop read the service. A procession of all the missionaries in their gowns, attended by the governor and all the officers of the garrison, followed our dear friend's remains to their last long resting place.

"Poor Duport, I do so pity him; but we must do all we can to comfort him. I have sent to inform him, but during such bad weather it is not easy to get communications with the Pongas. I hope he will soon come down, and then our bishop will think about ordaining him. His mission is in a very prosperous condition, and may the Lord of the harvest for Christ's sake raise up faithful men to labour in His harvest.

"Accept, my dear sir, of my kind Christian regards, and believe me to remain, yours very truly,

"FRANCIS POCOCK.

"To the Rev. H. Caswall."

Mr. Pocock's letter to Duport reached him at Fallangia in the course of a few weeks. Although dreadfully afflicted by the intelligence, he was supported by the hand of God, and wrote me the following letter:—

"Fallangia, Sept. 10.

"Reverend and dear Sir,

"This will bear to you the painful intelligence of the great loss which this mission has sustained by the removal of your much beloved friend and my pastor, the Rev. H. J. Leacock, from this world of misery and woe, to join the blessed company of the saints in glory—a time which he earnestly desired, and often would he say to me, 'John, I long to go home.' Yes, he has fought the good fight, he has finished his course, no more to be tossed on life's tempestuous sea. He had weathered out the storm; but now life's voyage is over. He laboured for his Lord and Master, and now he is entered into his rest. His threescore years are at an end; he was 'not ashamed of the Gospel of Jesus Christ;' he was a faithful servant of his Master whom he served, and in whose cause he died.

"This man of God braved the acclimating fever, and during that period of sufferings, great as they were, he still cast a glance at those of his unworthy assistant, and would strive to encourage him in the good errand on which they were sent.

"I am very sorry that I cannot do full justice to the labours of the departed; but I trust that some abler pen may undertake the task. I trust his friends in England and America will not grow cold. They could not give him a better memorial than to support the Mission which he has founded. I beg, for the sake of the deceased, your labour of love may not grow cold. Still exercise your efforts, and strive to stir up friends for us. I have not such influence as my reverend father in God had, but I know his desires, and I will strive to carry them out.

"On Sunday I lectured on the sad event, of which I heard a few days before. We had a large audience, and they listened with deep interest and profound silence, and at the close they burst forth in bitter grief, which would have melted an adamantine heart. Every eye was bathed with the tears of sorrow. In the afternoon I lectured on 'In my Father's house are many mansions,' &c., a portion of Scripture which was a favourite of the departed."

It was not Fallangia alone which bewailed the loss of the intrepid man of God. A newspaper (the "New Era,") published at Freetown, August 23, contained the following just tribute to his memory:—

"In affliction we naturally turn to those who have been similarly visited, and feel that in their hearts we touch a chord that vibrates in unison with our own. We trust, therefore, that it may prove a source of consolation to distant friends to be informed, that such has been the sensation in this city, created by the death of that most worthy and faithful servant of God, the Rev. H. J. Leacock, that we have not met with one individual capable of comprehending the sore bereavement the infant mission, of which he was the father, has been called to sustain, who does not deeply sympathize with them in the unexpected and deplorable removal of 'a burning and shining light' from this dark and benighted land.

266   SORROW IN SIERRA LEONE.

" The late Rev. Mr. Leacock, accompanied by his
very valuable assistant, Mr. Duport, arrived in this colony in the month of November, 1855, and lost no time
ere he decided on the theatre of his labours. The large
population of the numerous towns and villages on the
banks of the Rio Pongas appeared to present the most
distressing features of spiritual destitution, and to
offer an extensive and important field for missionary
exertion. Although the difficulties in encountering a
gross superstition in one of its strongholds, amidst the
swamps and morasses of a very pestilential river, trying to most constitutions, and particularly so to that
of an old man, amongst a people strongly tinctured
with an undying relish for the debasing slave trade,
sunk deep in the foulest degradation and the most
soul-destroying paganism, were facts well known and
duly weighed by Mr. Leacock; yet that venerable
servant had his Master's duty to execute, there was no
shrinking on his part, but facing the dangers with the
true courage of a faithful soldier of the Cross, he went
to his post; and his own hand has left us a record of
his successful efforts towards the fulfilment of the
work he had undertaken.

" The rev. gentleman suffered very severely from
fever, and was forced to return to this colony, where he
had been residing for some weeks, and to all human
foresight was rapidly regaining his health—indeed, we
believe he had so far progressed towards complete recovery as to have contemplated an early return to the
Pongas. ' Man proposes, but God disposes.' Mr.
Leacock was again prostrated, and after a few days

of suffering from fever and diarrhœa, on the 20th instant he was summoned to receive that crown made up of glory, honour, and immortality, leaving behind him a son in the ministry of the Church, and 'troops of friends,' with whom we have the sincerest sympathy in their sore bereavement.

"Few of those whose satisfaction it was to listen to the rev. gentleman's first address to a public assembly in this colony, on the subject of his visit to Africa, will have forgotten the fervid spirit of devotion and nervous energy of purpose which betrayed themselves in every sentence that fell from his lips, and made our hearts thrill with the liveliest emotions of hope for the old man's success.

"Whether we contemplate the labours of the late Mr. Leacock in the pulpit, on the platform, or in the mud hut on the banks of the Pongas, they all bear the impress of a truly missionary spirit. Mr. L. was very highly respected in this colony; and if other proof were wanting, we would point to the numerous and respectable attendance, including the governor, the clergy, officers of the garrison, and many of the principal inhabitants, that attended his remains from the cathedral to the grave, where the last rites were suitably performed by the Bishop of Sierra Leone.

"Mr. Leacock has left us a glorious example, which tells us that to end our earthly pilgrimage as he has done, is to meet him

" 'Where we may bathe the weary soul
In seas of heavenly rest,
And not a wave of trouble roll
Across the peaceful breast.' "

268 LETTER FROM THE BISHOP OF SIERRA LEONE.

The intelligence soon reached New York, and the "Church Journal" announced to the American Church that another martyr for Africa had entered into Paradise. Dr. Coit, writing to me from Troy, said of the deceased, "A purer mind and a truer heart than his, has seldom entered into the rest of the people of God. For him I rejoice, that his labours are all over, and that a boundless career of sinlessness and glory is all before him. I should have rejoiced to see his face once more; but my intimates are fast dropping away, and I must look to the natural end, and hope for joys far, far beyond it."

The Bishop of Sierra Leone wrote to the Bishop of Barbados the following letter :—

"Fourah Bay, September 11, 1856.

"My dear Lord Bishop,

"Very many circumstances have occurred in preventing my writing to you earlier, but I now feel that I am called upon by special circumstances to communicate with you. We have often, on the west coast of Africa, had cause to exercise faith in the Divine procedure—inscrutable and mysterious indeed are the ways of God to us. 'Be still, and know that I am God,' * is a lesson hard to be fully acquired.

"Your zealous and truly devoted servant, the Rev. H. J. Leacock, his health having failed at the Rio Pongas, came to this colony in May last for medical aid. At the time of his arrival here, I was

* Ps. xlvi. 10.

LETTER FROM THE BISHOP OF SIERRA LEONE. 269

laid aside by a severe fever, and therefore could not administer to his necessities. Our excellent and truly worthy friend, the Rev. F. Pocock (the assistant colonial chaplain) and his wife most kindly received him into their family, and nursed him as a brother. On my first visit to him on my recovery from the above illness, I was struck with the change which a few months had wrought in his general appearance. Dr. Bradshaw, our colonial surgeon, who was unremitting in his kind attention to Mr. Leacock, strongly advised his removal to Europe. To this step he was most reluctant, and we can well appreciate his motives for remaining on the coast. In the beginning of August we all had good hopes of his recovery, and for several weeks he gradually regained strength. So cheered was he in the prospect of once more returning to his dear little charge, that he told me, 'I have been making inquiry for a bell for my church and school, also a good boat, that I may visit the many towns on the banks of the rivers near Fallangia. I feel a degree of impatience, anxiously awaiting the termination of the rainy season, that I may return to my work.' In the mean time his heart was cheered by the receipt of letters from the old chief, Wilkinson, and letters and reports from Mr. Duport, which were of the most encouraging kind.

"I had promised Mr. Leacock that I would (God willing) pay a visit to his important charge during the next dry season, immediately after my return from the Yoruba country. I purpose going there by the November mail; probably I shall be absent from the colony three months. I hope to gain important information respecting the different tribes between Cape Coast Castle and Lagos, and I shall have sincere pleasure in acquainting your lordship with the result of my inquiries.

"On the 14th of August the Rev. H. J. Leacock was attacked with ague and fever, and on Sunday morning, the 17th, he was seized with severe diarrhœa, and from this time he was scarcely sensible. Every attention and kindness were shown him, but he gradually grew weaker until Wednesday, the 20th, when he fell asleep in Jesus.

"It would appear that this dear devoted servant of God had been for some time past ripening for glory. He expressed, some weeks since, an earnest desire to depart that he might be with Jesus, which he said was far better than remaining in this world of sin and sorrow. There is one circumstance in his case which does, I think, deserve particular attention, inasmuch as it marks the kind condescension of God to his faithful servants. Mr. Leacock had a dread of the last struggle with death, and how mercifully was he dealt with by his being insensible both to suffering and death for several days before his removal from time into eternity!

"Thus ends the short career of your first missionary to Africa. I feel that this most trying providence will be a severe blow to yourself and the honoured Committee of the West Indian Church Association for the Furtherance of the Gospel in Western Africa. But be not discouraged, the work is the

Lord's; it is for us to be faithful, it is with the Lord to bless. It will now devolve on your Committee to appoint a successor to him, whom God has thus early called to his reward. It is a great, arduous, and difficult task to carry on missionary work in the Rio Pangas and its neighbourhood. I earnestly pray that the Committee will be directed to the choice of a wise and faithful minister of the Gospel, to direct and superintend the operations of this new and important mission to the poor heathen.

Great respect was shown to the memory of our late brother. The governor and staff, the clergy in and near Freetown, many Europeans and natives, followed his remains from the cathedral to the new burial ground, and I performed the last solemn service. The change to him is a blessed one.

"I had arranged to see Mr. Duport the end of October or the beginning of November with a view to his ordination. But by Mr. Leacock's unexpected removal from us, I have made new arrangements, and sent to request Mr. Duport to come to the colony at his earliest convenience. I will gladly supply him both with cash for himself and necessaries for his schools, &c., until I hear from you, or your committee are able to make their own arrangements. It is now my intention, should Mr. Duport pass my examination satisfactorily (and I have every hope that he will), to ordain him both deacon and priest before he returns to the Rio Pongas. I quite hope that this plan will meet with the full approbation of your lordship, and of the committee.

272   LETTER FROM MR. WILKINSON.

"It will be perceived that the great necessity of the case has led me to adopt this resolution, to enable Mr. Duport to exercise the full office of the ministry of our Church among the people now to be placed under his charge, at least for some time to come.

"Two months since the governor and council voted unanimously £30 towards a second school in the Rio Pongas; and I have cheerfully added £10 for the same object from my diocesan fund. The late Rev. H. J. Leacock told me that he had engaged a schoolmaster to teach in this second school; I shall make further inquiry respecting him. While I am writing, the mail for England has arrived, and as I have many letters to send, you will excuse the abrupt conclusion of this communication.

"Sincerely praying for the Lord's guidance and blessing,

"I remain,

"Yours faithfully in the bonds of the Gospel,

"JOHN W. SIERRA LEONE.

"The Right Rev. the Lord Bishop of Barbados."

Four days after the Bishop Sierra Leone wrote this letter, the venerable chief of Fallangia, "the man of Macedonia," of our narrative, thus addressed the Bishop of Barbados :—

"Fallangia, September 15th, 1856.

"My Lord Bishop,

"After an elapse of time I have now taken up my pen with a trembling hand and sorrowful heart

THE SAD INTELLIGENCE REACHES BARBADOS. 273

to inform your lordship of the great loss we have sustained in our beloved champion of the Cross, the Rev. H. J. Leacock; and may the Great Disposer of all events raise many Leacocks in the West Indies to come over and help us poor miserable benighted Africans. John Duport has been doing his duty as a faithful steward of his Lord. I am now preparing material for the church and a mission-house; a school also shall be built. Our present congregation exceeds 100 souls, and scholars are offered every where, only a want of accommodation has prevented us from receiving them at the present. The harvest truly is plenteous, but the labourers are few; many are truly converted, and wish to be baptized, but there is no one here to do so at present. The whole of Fallangia have thrown away their greegrees and other superstitious rites, and many in our neighbourhood have done the same. They have foregone their follies, and Duport is still persevering in his labours; but his late imprudence has impaired his health through hard labour, but I have advised him not to overwork himself on any account in future. With due respects to your family, and accept of the same yourself,

"I remain, Sir,
"Your Lordship's humble servant,
"RICHARD WILKINSON."

When the sad tidings reached Mr. Leacock's native island, the sensation was most profound. The "Barbadian" newspaper appeared in mourning, its columns being lined with black as on the occasion of

274   EULOGY IN THE "BARBADIAN."

a public calamity. The following passages appeared under its editorial heading for November 5th and 8th :

"Words are wanting to describe the grief with which we lay before our readers the letters which the packet has this morning brought, and which will carry mourning and lamentation into many a household throughout this land, as well as in various other parts of the world. In the bitterness of our sorrow, however, we can still rejoice (God be praised for it) that our dear departed brother has joined the 'noble army of martyrs,' that he has died in the noblest of all causes, that we have given Africa, as a first instalment of the debt we owe her, our best, our bravest, our most well-beloved son.

"'The blood of the martyrs is the seed of the Church.' The man of God who has just 'gone to sleep in Afric's dust '—to quote his own words on the eve of his departure—has been privileged, before being called to his long home, to plant the standard of the Cross firmly, and, as we trust, immoveably in a corner of the land to whose spiritual welfare he had ardently devoted himself, body, soul, and spirit. The Rev. Hamble J. Leacock, the proto-martyr of the West Indian Church Association for the Furtherance of the Gospel in Western Africa, has gone to glory with a diadem of imperishable lustre on his brow. A more noble instance of self-sacrifice has never graced the annals of missionary enterprise. A more rapid success has hardly ever attended so short a career. If He who came to seek and to save that which was lost, in three short years achieved such incalculable

EULOGY IN THE "BARBADIAN." 275

good, that ' the world itself could not contain the books that should be written,' concerning his mighty deeds, his devoted servant, our Apostle to Africa, has at an humble distance followed his great Master's steps, and has been privileged in some degree to resemble Him in the astonishing results which attended the first preaching of the Cross to the heathens of Fallangia. Who can doubt that our dear departed brother was led by the Spirit into the moral wilderness to be welcomed in his declining years, and in a heathen land, with that noble 'Te Deum,' which burst on his astonished ears from the old chief Wilkinson, who declared that the Lord had sent Mr. Leacock in answer to the prayers he had offered for twenty years.

" Who can doubt that Providence directed our missionary to the very spot where he was to meet with this unexpected encouragement—an African chief, himself a Christian in heart, warmly welcoming him and seconding his efforts? Here is an old man, of great influence in the country, lodging and feeding our missionary, *at once* giving up the spacious piazza of his own abode as a temporary church, acting as interpreter, using his influence and authority to get together congregations, introducing neighbouring chiefs, encouraging the catechist's school, procuring pupils for it, and in fact furthering in every way the objects of the mission. Why it was enough to make good old Mr. Leacock respond to the 'Te Deum,' by exclaiming, 'Lord, now lettest thou thy servant depart in peace, for mine eyes have seen thy salvation!' Perhaps he *did* sing this song of triumph.

Like Moses on the top of Pisgah, he saw the land which God had promised him; with the eye of faith he realized the progress of the Gospel in the country of his adoption—the joy was too great for him, he felt his own nothingness in view of so great a work, of so great a privilege, and he could not help desiring to depart and be with Christ, which was far better! We learn indeed from the painfully-interesting and affecting letter of the Bishop of Sierra Leone, that a few days before his death he *had* expressed a desire of this sort, although he had not long before showed a great eagerness to return to his work.

"Dreadful as is the blow to us, disappointed as we all are at being denied the privilege of welcoming him back amongst us, and hearing from his own lips the tidings of his mission, the providence of God may, and we trust will overrule the sad event for the ultimate good of the mission; the very eagerness and liking for the good news, which was manifested so unmistakeably by many, may be stimulated by his removal. We shall be much mistaken if the Joshua who succeeds him, and who promises so worthily to follow his steps, does not soon rally around him a devoted band of followers, whose reception of and adherence to the Gospel shall gladden his heart, bring peace and happiness to themselves, and encourage those who, in various parts of the world, are joining together to promote this holy work.

"We do not grudge Africa our Leacock: we entertain a holy envy of her for the privilege she enjoys of cherishing his ashes; and if we had a hundred

CONCLUDING LETTER FROM MR. DUPORT. 277

more such sons, we would gladly give them to her!
But she does not need them; she has sons of her own;
she has her Duports, who can do all that our Leacocks
could do for her, and more—because they can stand the
climate better. We will train and teach them, and
send them to her, and then bid her and them God
speed!"

This memoir cannot, perhaps, be better concluded
than by a letter to the writer from Mr. Duport (now
the Rev. John Henry A. Duport), written within
three weeks after the decease of his friend and pastor:—

"The fields are white already for harvest. There
are *four* places ready now to receive missionary stations. Our congregation has increased to upwards
of one hundred attentive hearers. We have no room
for the people, and this is during the rains. I am
very happy also to inform you that they have cast
away all their idolatry and the gods in which they
once placed implicit confidence. Many brought theirs
to me. They are very anxious to be baptized. They
are fully convinced of their errors, and many are
striving to become faithful servants of Christ. Some
come the distance of four miles through the heavy
rains to hear the word of God. I went to see a woman who was very sick indeed, and I sent her some
medicine. To my great surprise she attended evening
service, and when asked why she ventured out in the
damp, she replied, 'I feel little better, and I wanted
to come to hear what God say.' Mr. Wilkinson has

already begun to gather materials for the building. He says nothing shall deter him from the work, that he is only waiting until the rains cease. Many of our little congregation attend the Sunday school, who most earnestly wish to read the Bible, 'from which they hear such good things.'

"The school children number thirty-two at present; every one is doing well. Two of the boys I took in their pure wild state are now able to read the Prayer Book; their writing is good, their memory retentive. They know the Lord's Prayer, the Ten Commandments, and the Creed, in English and in their own tongue. I have, with the assistance of Mr. Wilkinson, translated some of the reading sentences at the commencement of the service, the Lord's Prayer, and the prayers after it, the Te Deum, Creed and prayers after, the Ten Commandments and the responses, and a part of the Sunday School Primer.

"I am very happy to inform you that our labours have not been in vain in this place. Our mission is making rapid progress, and making lasting impressions (I hope) on the minds of the people. Many express how they have been deceived by the Mohammedans. They very willingly pay for their books and those of their children, in produce: Mr. Wilkinson is a very great help to me.

"One man who was a zealous attendant, and the first to cast away his greegrees, is now no more. The last night he was permitted to join us, after service he took his handkerchief and blindfolded his eyes, and said, 'If I had died before the missionaries came

here, I would have died in darkness, but now I see.'
He went home and was never permitted to return.

"I was called to go and see him very soon, and I met him suffering very much. His appearance was already changed, and I had very poor hopes of his recovery. He was about seventy years of age. I conversed with him and asked him many questions, to each of which he gave very satisfactory answers. He said his whole trust was in God and in his Son Jesus Christ, and that he had committed himself to his care and protection (I had an interpreter).

"On the Sunday after, I went to see him, and pointed him to the only way of salvation, Jesus Christ. He replied, 'Da he me a look to, me pray to Him night and day.' I prayed with him, and repeated the Lord's Prayer in his own tongue. When I was ready to leave, he grasped my hands firmly and most heartily replied, '*Allah etantoo*' (God bless you), and ere I reached home he sent presents to me. I never saw his face again.

"It was a custom of the country, that when the husband dies, the wives and all who are connected with the place are accused of having by witchcraft taken his life. This act the old man prohibited on his death-bed. He said (I was told), 'I am about to die, let no one accuse my people of witchcraft, no one has done me any thing, I die by the hand of God.' Many have been the convictions which have taken place, although our mission is in its infant state. A few weeks ago, one evening after service, a man said to Mr. Wilkinson, 'Master, this is the greegree we want, God's book is the best greegree, greegree for all, old and young, this is the best of greegrees.'

"The people are very kind, although very poor. They love to hear of Jesus Christ, they love to hear of heaven and learn the way to it. Old and young are desirous of learning to read. They will have nothing to do with the Mohammedans, they look upon them as their enemies. One man who was a greegree worshipper, one day took up the book of another man who belongs to us ; the latter snatched the book from him and said, ' Do not put your hands on my book, because you are a greegree worshipper, and have greegree in your cap.' The former joined us about three weeks since.

" We keep service every night, and three times on Sundays, with Sunday school. Twenty-two adults attend the Sunday school. The whole Sabbath is dedicated to the Lord. Surely the Lord has visited his people here, and has blessed our labours with abundant success. Surely the deceased has not left his home and comforts for nought. His name will be handed down to posterity for ages yet to come.

" May God bless you, and grant you long life. That you may do a great deal of good for the cause of missions is the sincere wish of your humble and devoted servant,

" JOHN HENRY A. DUPORT."

FUNERAL ANTHEM.

Brother, thou art gone before us, and thy saintly soul is flown
Where tears are wiped from every eye, and sorrow is unknown;
From the burthen of the flesh, and from care and fear released,
Where the wicked cease from troubling, and the weary are at rest.

The toilsome way thou'st travelled o'er, and borne the heavy load,
But Christ hath taught thy languid feet to reach his blest abode ;
Thou'rt sleeping now, like Lazarus, upon his father's breast,
Where the wicked cease from troubling, and the weary are at rest.

Sin can never taint thee now, nor doubt thy faith assail,
Nor thy meek faith in Jesus Christ and the Holy Spirit fail ;
And there thou'rt sure to meet the good, whom on earth thou lovedst
        best,
Where the wicked cease from troubling, and the weary are at rest.

'Earth to earth,' and ' dust to dust,' the solemn priest hath said,
So we lay the turf above thee now, and we seal thy narrow bed:
But thy spirit, brother, soars away among the faithful blest,
Where the wicked cease from troubling, and the weary are at rest.

And when the Lord shall summon us, whom thou hast left behind,
May we, untainted by the world, as sure a welcome find;
May each, like thee, depart in peace, to be a glorious guest,
Where the wicked cease from troubling, and the weary are at rest.

THE END.

VALUABLE AND INTERESTING WORKS

RECENTLY PUBLISHED BY

THOMAS N. STANFORD,

637 BROADWAY.

History of the African Mission

Of the Protestant Episcopal Church in the United States; with Memoirs of Deceased Missionaries, and Notices of Native Customs.

BY MRS. E. F. HENING.

1 vol. 12mo. Cloth. 75 cents.

This work, based upon the details of missionary journals, is replete with interest. It also comprises historical notices of the origin and progress of the African Missions, together with biographical sketches of its missionaries, &c. The work embodies a large amount of highly interesting and valuable information relating to the country and the habits of its people. The author was herself a missionary.

Scenes in our Parish.

BY A COUNTRY PARSON'S DAUGHTER.

(MRS. MARCUS H. HOLMES.)

To which is prefixed a Memoir of the Author, by her Sister.

12mo. Cloth. $1.

Rev. Chas. B. Tayler's Works.

10 vols. 12mo. Cloth. 75 cents each. Sold separately.

MARK WILTON,
SCENES IN CLERGYMAN'S LIFE,
THE ANGELS' SONG,
MARGARET, OR THE PEARL.
THANKFULNESS,

RECORDS OF A GOOD MAN'S LIFE,
TRUTH, OR PERSIS CLARETON,
LADY MARY, or Not of the World
EARNESTNESS,
LEGENDS AND RECORDS.

These beautiful productions have passed through numerous editions, both in this country and in England. Excellent in their design and teaching, they have been welcomed with the heartiest commendation by the Press universally.

———◆———

History of the Reformation in England.

BY REV. J. A. SPENCER, D. D.

18mo. Cloth. 50 cents.

A comprehensive and carefully digested epitome of the great era of Reform in the Church of England.

———◆———

Colton's Genius and Mission
OF THE PROTESTANT EPISCOPAL CHURCH IN THE UNITED STATES.

BY THE LATE REV. CALVIN COLTON, LL. D.

———◆———

The Connections of the Universe,
As Seen in the Light of God's Created and Written Revelations.

1 vol. 12mo. Muslin. $1.

"This is an able and excellent work. Its aim is to show the connections between the Revelation of God, in the Creation, the Bible, and the life of Christ; and to show, in all the manifestations, the same Infinite and Divine Mind. The author treats his subject with originality and vigor, and in a way well calculated to produce a deep and truthful impression upon the common mind."—*Courier & Enquirer.*

T. N. STANFORD'S VALUABLE PUBLICATIONS. 3

Bp. Brownell's Commentary
ON THE BOOK OF COMMON PRAYER, &c.
Historical, Explanatory, Doctrinal, and Practical.
New Revised Edition, royal 8vo. Cloth. $3.

This elaborate and able work, which combines the fullest historical illustration of the Book of Common Prayer, has long been acknowledged as a standard authority. It is an invaluable compendium of the best English writers on the subject of the Liturgy. The aim of this noble production is to exhibit the full import of its several offices to those who, from habitual use, may sometimes fail to catch the inspiration of that deep spirit of piety which should animate them.

LECTURES UPON
Historical Portions of Old Testament.
By ARCHDEACON BETHUNE, of YORK, ENG.
12mo. Cloth. 75 cents.

An admirable book, designed for Sabbath reading in the family circle. Its aim is to induce a more intimate acquaintance with Bible history and biography.

CONTENTS.—Sodom and Gomorrah—Passage of the Red Sea—The Daughters of Moab—Death of Sisera—Saul made King—David numbering the People—Naboth and Ahab—The Shunammite and her Son—Naaman, the Syrian—Sickness of King Hezekiah—Shadrack, Meshack, and Abednego—Jonah's Flight—Repentance of the Ninevites, &c.

Memoirs of Mrs. Elizabeth Fry,
Including an Account of her Labors in Promoting the Reformation
of Female Prisoners, and the Improvement of British Seamen.
By THE REV. THOMAS TIMPSON.
12mo. 75 cents.

Domestic and Religious Life in Italy;
Or, the Confessions of a Convert to Romanism.
EDITED BY THE RT. REV. W. J. KIP, D. D.
16mo. 63 cents.

T. N. STANFORD'S
THEOLOGICAL BOOK STORE,
637 BROADWAY.
(LATE STANFORD & SWORDS.)

AT this Establishment will be found a large and valuable collection of Standard Works in

THEOLOGY, PHILOSOPHY, CRITICISM, SCIENCE, BIOGRAPHY, TRAVELS, POETRY,

and the other branches of General Literature, including all the NEW PUBLICATIONS OF THE DAY.

Just received, a new importation of very choice and exceedingly rare

WORKS ON SACRED LITERATURE,

to which the attention of the Clergy and Laity is respectfully solicited. These valuable productions are now on view.

STANFORD'S
Sacred Selections, or Literary Indicator.

A guide to the choice of the best books, with characteristic extracts, is now ready for distribution gratuitously; also, the new Catalogue of Stanford's Publications in Theological and General Literature.

SCARCE AND VALUABLE WORKS IMPORTED TO ORDER,
FOR PUBLIC OR PRIVATE LIBRARIES,
DIRECT FROM THE LONDON AGENTS.

The Standard and authorized Editions of
THE BOOK OF COMMON PRAYER.

The attention of the clergy and the religious public is respectfully invited to Stanford's elegant series of editions of the Book of Common Prayer and Church Lessons, consisting of about twenty different sizes and styles of type, from the folio, printed in large English type suitable for the Altar, to the miniature editions for private use, combining the advantages of portability with distinctness.

The utmost care and attention have been given to render this series unsurpassed by any thing in this department hitherto attempted in the United States. Elegance in typography, the best fabric of paper, and the latest improvements in binding, have been secured, for imparting the utmost artistic perfection to these editions; and the test of their superiority is therefore confidently referred to the discriminating taste of the community.

The various styles of binding in morocco, gilt, antique, flexible and plain, also in velvet, ivory inlaid, with clasps, etc., will be found well worthy inspection. The series also includes editions in plain binding of unexampled neatness and cheapness.

T. N. STANFORD, 637 *Broadway*,
(LATE STANFORD & SWORDS.)

Trieste

Trieste Publishing has a massive catalogue of classic book titles. Our aim is to provide readers with the highest quality reproductions of fiction and non-fiction literature that has stood the test of time. The many thousands of books in our collection have been sourced from libraries and private collections around the world.

The titles that Trieste Publishing has chosen to be part of the collection have been scanned to simulate the original. Our readers see the books the same way that their first readers did decades or a hundred or more years ago. Books from that period are often spoiled by imperfections that did not exist in the original. Imperfections could be in the form of blurred text, photographs, or missing pages. It is highly unlikely that this would occur with one of our books. Our extensive quality control ensures that the readers of Trieste Publishing's books will be delighted with their purchase. Our staff has thoroughly reviewed every page of all the books in the collection, repairing, or if necessary, rejecting titles that are not of the highest quality. This process ensures that the reader of one of Trieste Publishing's titles receives a volume that faithfully reproduces the original, and to the maximum degree possible, gives them the experience of owning the original work.

We pride ourselves on not only creating a pathway to an extensive reservoir of books of the finest quality, but also providing value to every one of our readers. Generally, Trieste books are purchased singly - on demand, however they may also be purchased in bulk. Readers interested in bulk purchases are invited to contact us directly to enquire about our tailored bulk rates. Email: customerservice@triestepublishing.com

You May Also Like

ISBN: 9780649637270
Paperback: 50 pages
Dimensions: 6.14 x 0.10 x 9.21 inches
Language: eng

The Little Dream: An Allegory in Six Scenes. [1911]

John Galsworthy

ISBN: 9780649724185
Paperback: 130 pages
Dimensions: 6.14 x 0.28 x 9.21 inches
Language: eng

Report of the Second Annual Meeting of the Maryland State Bar Association, Held at Ocean City, Maryland, July 28-29, 1897

Conway W. Sams

www.triestepublishing.com

You May Also Like

ISBN: 9780649587667
Paperback: 176 pages
Dimensions: 6.14 x 0.38 x 9.21 inches
Language: eng

Second Year Language Reader

Franklin T. Baker & George R. Carpenter & Katharine B. Owen

ISBN: 9780649640430
Paperback: 332 pages
Dimensions: 6.14 x 0.69 x 9.21 inches
Language: eng

The Works of James Russell Lowell, Vol. VII. The Poetical Works of James Russell Lowell, in Four Volumes, Vol. I

James Russell Lowell

www.triestepublishing.com

You May Also Like

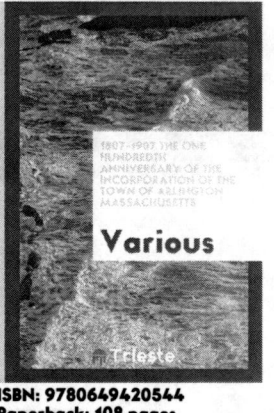

ISBN: 9780649420544
Paperback: 108 pages
Dimensions: 6.14 x 0.22 x 9.21 inches
Language: eng

1807-1907 The One Hundredth Anniversary of the incorporation of the Town of Arlington Massachusetts

Various

ISBN: 9780649194292
Paperback: 44 pages
Dimensions: 6.14 x 0.09 x 9.21 inches
Language: eng

Biennial report of the Board of State Harbor Commissioners, for the two fiscal years commencing July 1, 1890, and ending June 30, 1892

Various

www.triestepublishing.com

You May Also Like

Biennial report of the Board of State Harbor Commissioners for the two fisca years. Commeneing July 1, 1884, and Ending June 30, 1886

Various

ISBN: 9780649199693
Paperback: 48 pages
Dimensions: 6.14 x 0.10 x 9.21 inches
Language: eng

Biennial report of the Board of state commissioners, for the two fiscal years, commencing July 1, 1890, and ending June 30, 1892

Various

ISBN: 9780649196395
Paperback: 44 pages
Dimensions: 6.14 x 0.09 x 9.21 inches
Language: eng

Find more of our titles on our website. We have a selection of thousands of titles that will interest you. Please visit

www.triestepublishing.com

CPSIA information can be obtained
at www.ICGtesting.com
Printed in the USA
LVOW07s2103071017
551578LV00003B/154/P